The Splendor of Persia

The Splendor of
PERSIA

by Robert Payne

ILLUSTRATED WITH LINE DECORATIONS
BY Leonard Everett Fisher
AND WITH PHOTOGRAPHS

New York : Alfred A. Knopf : 1957

L. C. catalog card number: 57–9202

© ROBERT PAYNE, 1957

THIS IS A BORZOI BOOK,
PUBLISHED BY ALFRED A. KNOPF, INC.

FIRST EDITION

FOR

Abdol Hossein Hamzavi

Blessed is he who feeds at the well-spring:

for the sum of honor is the water of life.

Acknowledgments

I WISH *to express my deepfelt gratitude to my teachers—Professor Arthur Upham Pope, Chancellor Emeritus of the Asia Institute, New York, who kindly read through my manuscript and granted me permission to reproduce illustrations from* Masterpieces of Persian Art, An Introduction to Persian Art, *and* A Survey of Persian Art; *to Dr. Phyllis Ackerman, who most generously read through the chapter on "The Divine Radiance"; and to Mr. Joseph V. McMullan, M.A., who gave me at all times free access to his vast honeycomb of knowledge of Persian carpets.*

Contents

List of Photographs

The Splendor of Persia

The Land and the People

$\mathcal{I}$F YOU look at a modern map of Persia, you will see how it stretches like a great arrowhead from the Caspian Sea to the Indian Ocean, and lies between India and Russia. Afghanistan, the Turkmen Republic, Turkey, Iraq, and Saudi Arabia are its neighbors. Then turn to an ancient map—such a map as the Emperor

Darius, "the King of Kings," might have looked upon twenty-four centuries ago—and you will see the Persian Empire stretching into the eastern Mediterranean, including large parts of Greece and all of Egypt, and reaching out to include vast areas of southern Russia and making deep inroads into Central Asia, Pakistan, and northern India. The Persian Empire swallowed up the Babylonian and Assyrian Empires, and went beyond them. It was the greatest empire the world had ever known, and for two centuries its capital was the capital of the world. Today only the core of this empire remains. But the Persians, who rarely regret the past, do not believe the glory has departed. Speaking quite confidently, as though it were the most natural thing in the world, they will say: "Glory lay over this land from the beginning."

For them Persia is far more than a country: it is a place of splendor, where the gods dwell and the ancient heroes still walk in the land, where the remote past and the immediate present live side by side. For them all other lands are disappointing, for the sun does not shine so brightly elsewhere and there are almost no buildings beyond the boundaries of Persia which shine so brightly as their blue-tiled mosques. The Persian sky, scintillating with the dust of the vast deserts or washed clean by the heavy rains, makes everything appear brighter than it really is. Outlines are sharper, colors clearer, shadows more sombre than elsewhere. It is a country of violent contrasts, the snow mountains

THE SPLENDOR OF PERSIA

looking down on endless deserts, bitter cold and intense heat, Switzerland and Arabia stirred together.
Two thirds of Persia is mountain and desert. It is no
wonder that the Persians in their rare oases have a passionate love for gardens.

The mountains and the deserts formed the Persians:
the glittering snows, the endless empty spaces of the
desert where nothing grows and no animals can live
have formed their minds and toughened their spirits.
They have the hardiness of mountaineers and the contemplative instincts of the desert-dwellers. There is
nothing essentially Asiatic about them: they are the
Europeans of the East, with high foreheads, straight
noses, and fresh coloring. They are Aryans, and today
they call their country Iran, which is only another way
of spelling Aryan. Because they originally spoke an
Aryan tongue, even today their language is close to ours
in feeling and a surprising number of words are common to Persian and English. But if they can be compared with any other race, we must turn to the French,
who have the same dancing attitude to life, the same
quick wits, the same love for decoration, the same
sense of glory and splendor. There are moments, walking in Teheran, when you can almost imagine yourself
in some southern French town near the Pyrenees.

Glory, splendor . . . these are the words which
come most often to one's lips in describing the Persians. Partly, of course, it derives from the memory of
the great empires which spread out of Persia, the lux-

THE LAND AND THE PEOPLE

ury of the courts, the palaces flashing with jewels, Haroun al-Raschid, Persepolis, the Thousand and One Nights:

> *Is it not passing brave to be a King*
> *And ride in triumph through Persepolis?*

But it is worth remembering that the Greeks, who fought the Persians to a standstill and under Alexander finally conquered them, considered them to be the most splendid of mortals. Herodotus, who described them lovingly and in great detail, his famous *History* being essentially a History of Persia with occasional references to neighboring states, delighted in their long, rolling, splendid names, "which are like their bodies and their magnificence." He noted accurately that all their names ended in sibilants: it was like the clang of metal on metal. Xenophon, who fought in the Persian army, regarded Cyrus, the founder of the Achaemenian dynasty, as the greatest of all Kings, the model for all to come, a man so wise that he was almost a god, and so human that it was impossible not to feel an overwhelming affection for him. Xenophon described him as the most handsome of men, lithe and tall, equally at ease on his throne of hammered gold or moving about the camp, at horseplay with his soldiers. He laughed easily and had a ready wit, he possessed astonishing physical strength and employed every artifice of cunning to defeat his enemies, and in all this he was so like what the Greeks

THE SPLENDOR OF PERSIA

wanted to be that they were inclined to regard him almost as one of themselves.

What the Greeks admired most among the Persians was a peculiar combination of magnificence and simplicity, a quality which has been evident in their art and in their characters through all ages. The Persians taught their boys three things—to ride the horse, to shoot with the bow, and to tell the truth. They thought it dishonorable for a man to be in debt, because they believed that a man in debt generally tells lies. They possessed another quality which was rare among the Greeks: an intense loyalty to their King, who could do no wrong in their eyes. They elevated the King to a place of utmost splendor, showered him with gifts, exalted him above all men, seeing in the King an image of their own magnificence. In this sense the Persians were the inventors of monarchy. Other nations had had Kings, who ruled by terror, by brute force, by divine right. The Persians were the first to establish a tradition of Kingship based upon joyful consent.

Above all the Greeks admired the sturdy courage of the Persians. Herodotus says that in the last great battle of the Persian War the Persians fought with a strength and a spirit to match the Spartans, but the Spartans were in armor and the Persians in linen shirts. They were better at shooting with their bows than with lances and swords, and their gold coins show an image of the King as an archer.

If the Persians were the first world-conquerors, they

THE LAND AND THE PEOPLE

were also among the most tolerant empire-builders the world has ever seen. They worshipped the god Ahuramazda, Lord of the Sun and of the Shining Heavens, but they never attempted to proselytize and allowed astonishing freedom of self-government among the subject peoples. They released the Jews from the Babylonian captivity, restored their ritual vessels and assisted them to rebuild the Temple. They even rebuilt the walls from Athens to the Piraeus which the Spartans had levelled. For over two centuries they maintained a world of law, peace and justice over an area which extended from the Indus and the Oxus to the Nile and the Aegean. When the Greeks spoke of the Persians, it was always with awe mingled with envy and the desire to imitate. When Alexander the Great became master of the Persian Empire, he assumed quite naturally the robes and the powers of the Persian Emperors and consorted more with Persians than with Greeks. He borrowed the design of a world-empire from Darius, and modelled himself on Cyrus. There was nothing capricious in his choice of a model. There is a sense in which the wars between the Greeks and the Persians were civil wars, fought by two superbly gifted peoples of the same race.

If by some magical means we could be transported to Persia at the time of Darius, what kind of people would we see? It happens that we know the answer, because hundreds of portraits of Persians survive at Persepolis, carved in long relief on the great stairway, and the faces we see there are the same faces we

THE SPLENDOR OF PERSIA

see today in Isfahan and Shiraz, and even more in the mountain villages. Again we see those faces in the carvings of the Sasanians, who reigned a thousand years after Darius. We recognize them again in the thousands of portraits that have survived from the time of the Emperor Shah Abbas, who ruled over Persia during the reign of England's Queen Elizabeth. There is an extraordinary continuity in the Persian face: lean, intense, with wide eyes, firm chin, delicate nostrils, and with the suggestion of a strange inner excitement. So little has changed that sometimes you have the feeling that the people are only waiting to step back into the remote, unobtainable and dazzling past. Every morning the Teheran radio begins the day's work with a recitation from a poetic epic on the ancient Persian heroes —the *Shah Nameh* of Firdausi. It is almost as though the British radio were to begin every morning with a recitation from *Beowulf*.

There are good reasons for the continuity of Persian features and Persian character. Invaders have swept over the land: Arabs, Mongols, Greeks, Turks, and Scythians. They came in floods, stayed for a little while, and then the floods subsided, leaving the original Persians unharmed. Again and again in Persian history we come upon periods of confused wars, with perhaps ten armies rampaging across the country: then the smoke clears, and we discover there is a new Emperor on the throne claiming descent from the ancient Achaemenian Emperors. After periods of confusion, the ancient and familiar patterns of government

THE LAND AND THE PEOPLE

emerge again. Even today, in the reign of Mohammad Reza Shah Pahlavi, we can observe patterns of government which derive from the time of Darius. In any other country such a fantastic continuity would be a sign of weakness: in Persia it is a sign of strength.

Given the nature of the land, this continuity is easily explained. It is a hard and bitter land, with few rivers and few trees except in the Caspian provinces. Here quite suddenly on a narrow strip of shore, the normal order of nature in Persia is reversed. Here swiftly flowing rivers drop from the high mountains into an inland sea, and there are rich agricultural lands and vast forests teeming with game. As a consequence Mazanderan and Gilan on the shores of the Caspian Sea have tempted raiders from the time of the Vikings in the tenth century to the Bolsheviks in 1920. The principal granary of Persia is a thin strip of land to the north, hidden from the rest of the country by the high ranges of the Elburz mountains which extend from the Caucasus to Afghanistan.

In a land so poor in natural resources, it was inevitable that the Persians, like the Scots, should become intensely clannish; inevitable that they should adopt feudal ways and swear oaths of absolute obedience to their feudal lords and their Kings; inevitable that they should resist change. When conquered by the Arabs and forced to submit to Islam, the Persians accepted the new religion imposed upon them and immediately set about changing Islamic law and Islamic custom to suit their own character, with the result that nearly all

THE SPLENDOR OF PERSIA

Persians belong to a branch of Islam which is regarded as heretical in Cairo and in Mecca. The chief annual holiday is still the New Year Festival at the coming of spring, as it was in the time of Darius. The Persians have preserved their national characteristics, but they may still have to pay a heavy price for this luxury which they can hardly afford in the present world.

An Englishman returning to the England of five hundred years ago would hardly recognize the land, so much has it changed as a result of enclosure, new crops, and new farming methods. A modern Persian returning to the Persia of two thousand years ago would find little changed. There are places even now where the peasants farm their fields with the same primitive implements they used thousands of years ago, and the peasants wear the same felt caps and loose cloaks which can be seen carved on the Persepolis stairway. They live, as they have always lived, in mud huts in small villages which belong to landlords who may never have set eyes on their property. Each village has its headman, or *kadkhuda*, appointed by the landlord to manage the estate.

The produce of the land is divided into five parts, one part to the peasant who provides the water, another to the owner of the draft animals, another to the owner of the seed, another to the labor force, and another to the landlord. It may happen that the headman possesses the draft animals, the seed and the water rights, so that the village peasants have only a fifth of the land's produce to divide among themselves.

THE LAND AND THE PEOPLE

This division of the wealth of the land is known to have existed before the Islamic Conquest of the seventh century. Usually the peasant is in debt to the landlord, without any hope of ever being released from debt. Unscrupulous landlords present an almost insoluble problem to an administration determined to change the laws of land tenure.

It is characteristic of Persia that the movement to return the land to the peasants is led by the largest landowner of all, the Shah-in-Shah, who has distributed crown lands against the wishes of the feudal landowners. Meanwhile the peasants' lot is still a grim one. There is never enough water, even though the agricultural areas of Persia are supplied with excellent subterranean canals called *qanats*. There is never enough rainfall and never enough good land. The land is still as rugged as it ever was; the mountains have not changed; and the deserts with their salt craters reminiscent of the moon's surface seen through a telescope still threaten the peasants. What is surprising is that a country so barren and unrewarding until the discovery of oil should have produced so many great poets and artists, and to have extended its cultural influence far beyond its present political frontiers. It is almost as though the Persian imagination, so rich and warm, were brought into being to compensate for the stark poverty of the land.

"All Persians are artists," said the Shah-in-Shah recently. He might have added that they are also all poets. Shepherds and wandering tribesmen can recite whole books of the ancient epics and kitchen-maids know the poems of Sa'di and Hafiz, the two most beloved poets of Persia, while every Persian with any pretension to culture is a poet. While poetry has been the main force responsible for keeping Persian traditions alive, it is mother wit which helps the Persians to face the present. In the early years of the last century James Morier, the British representative at the court of Persia, wrote a book called *The Adventures of Hajji Baba of Isfahan.* Hajji Baba is always putting his nose into affairs that do not concern him, and always getting involved in difficulties from which he extricates himself by a triumphant display of wit and resourcefulness. He is no respecter of persons. He talks with Kings as insolently as he talks with women, landlords, and viziers. Gregarious and friendly, he scorns the world's malice and comes up laughing in the end. Persians are sometimes inclined to regard the book with suspicion, on the grounds that it gives too many of their secrets away. No one who has ever been to Persia can forget the fierce gentleness of their wit and their addiction to stories so adroitly embroidered that the teller is drowned in the embroidery.

It is partly the fault of the language, which is soft and resonant and tends to carry the speaker away into the wildest improvizations, a language wonderfully suited to the audacious. This crisp and enticing language convinces easily: as musical as Italian and as neat as French. Americans who say they know no Persian know more than they think they know. Over a

THE LAND AND THE PEOPLE

hundred and fifty English words have been borrowed from the Persian. Here are sixty words in common use which we have taken from them:

azure	jasmine	naphtha	satrap
bazaar	jasper	narcissus	scarlet
candy	julep	orange	scimitar
caravan	jungle	palanquin	seersucker
cheque	khaki	paradise	shawl
chess	lemon	peach	sherbet
cinnabar	lilac	peacock	spinach
cypress	lime	pear	sugar
dervish	Magi	puttee	taffeta
divan	magic	pajama	tapestry
exchequer	margarine	rice	tiara
gazelle	marguerite	rook	tiger
henna	muscadel	saccharine	tulip
jackal	musk	saffron	turban
jargon	myrtle	sash	verandah

If you will say some of these words softly, with a slight singsong intonation, you will have some idea of the sound of Persian, a language curiously like English, having many words which we share with them. *Mother* is *mader*, *father* is *pedar*, *brother* is *barader*. *Two* is *do*, *six* is *shesh*, *is* is *ist*. Persian belongs to the great group of Indo-Aryan languages, our own language being the very last to be developed. Coming back to Persian is like coming back to the source.

Like English, Persian is a language which cries out for poets: there has been no dearth of poetry in Persia.

THE SPLENDOR OF PERSIA

Unfortunately the Persian poet most familiar in the West is one of the least typical. Omar Khayyám is recognized in his own country as an excellent mathematician and astronomer, and the hero of some curious legends, but he is given no very high place as a poet. Edward Fitzgerald's translation of the *Rubaiyat* describes only one aspect of the Persian character: their love of wine and women, a raw anguish at the thought of the impermanence of the world. In English the poem has the sound of trumpets, but in the original Persian it has more of the sound of muffled drums, a slow lament. So it is that nearly all translations from Persian fail: we miss the softness of the Persian syllables and the sound like running waters that goes through all their poetry. We miss much in an English version of the *Rubaiyat*, and forget that when he is talking about the Tavern he means the House of Love, and when he is talking about grapes and wine, he means the Truth which God pours out upon the heads of men, though he also means real grapes pressed into real wine—for the poem is to be read on many levels. We do gain at moments an astonishing insight into the Persian character with its defiance, its sense of the splendor of the visible world and its mysticism and reliance upon God, at once in this world and out of it. And though Omar Khayyám is not typical, and he is often pedestrian in the *Rubaiyat*, there are moments when he is completely convincing, as when he celebrates the Prophet Mohammad:

THE LAND AND THE PEOPLE

The mighty Mahmud, the victorious Lord,
That all the misbelieving and black Horde
Of fears and sorrows that inflict the soul
Scatters and slays with his enchanted Sword.

It is the typical Persian attitude towards Mohammad, in whose name they were conquered by the Arabs. Refusing to accept orthodox Islam, they transformed it into something closer to their heart's desire and clothed it in enchantment. They turned orthodox Islam upside down, spun fairy tales around it, elevated Ali, the son-in-law of the Prophet, almost above the Prophet himself, and came to believe in time that the sacred cities of Islam were in Persia itself. In their poetry enchanted swords are everywhere.

We owe a debt to Persia we can never repay. So much that is bright and glittering and desirable was invented by them. They were the first to invent angels, which the Jews borrowed during the Babylonian captivity, and the Christians borrowed from the Jews. The most beautiful of all decorated domes are in Persia. They invented chess and polo, and the first known highways for wheeled traffic were the royal roads built by Darius. And half our fairy tales have Persian origins. Their intellectual and spiritual contributions to the world derive from the enchanted interpretation of the world they saw before their eyes: for them the world was a flame, forever quivering, forever bright, forever leaping. For them the world was magic. The very word *magic* comes from their fire-worship-

THE SPLENDOR OF PERSIA

Pope

ISFAHAN. Mosque of the Shah, Portal to Sanctuary. *Period of Shah Abbas.*

ISFAHAN. Mosque of the Shah, Portal to Sanctuary. *Period of Shah Abbas.*

ISFAHAN. Haroun ar Valiat. *Early nineteenth century.*

Isfahan. Mosque of Sheykh Lutfullah. *Period of Shah Abbas*

[opposite] Detail of Carpet made in Tabriz. *Period of Shah Abbas.*

Medallion Carpet. Garden in center, surrounded by paradisiacal hunting ground. *Period of Shah Abbas.*

ISFAHAN. Chihil Sutun. Audience Palace of Shah Abbas.

ISFAHAN. The Meidan-i-Shah, showing the Mosque of the Shah and
Ali Qapu on right.

Tomb at Abarquh, *dated 1056* A.D.

Brass Ewer engraved with silver and copper, *dated 1232* A.D.

Engraved Silver Plate, with Bahram I as Prince Royal, *about 272* A.D.

Taq-i-Bustan. Shapur I receiving royal ring in the presence of
Zarathustra.

Tomb of Cyrus at PASARGADAE.

The Palaces at PERSEPOLIS.

PERSEPOLIS. Reliefs on Apadana stairway.

Rhyton with Griffin end. *Achaemenian.*

PERSEPOLIS. Apadana stairway. Lion and Bull.

Metropolitan Museum

Head of early Persian Prince, *pre-Achaemenian.*

Government of Iran

Head of Parthian General from Shami.

ping priests, the Magi who attended upon Xerxes and Darius. And remembering the Magi who attended the birth of Christ, the third-century theologian Sextus Julius Africanus wrote: "Our first knowledge of Jesus came from Persia."

We shall understand Persia best by looking at her long history, where the rise and decline of four great dynasties seems always to follow the same pattern, as though the Persians themselves had remained unchanged through all recorded time, reacting in the same way to the challenges thrown down by succeeding dynasties. And as we look at their history unfolding before us, it seems sometimes that there is little change: Xerxes and Shapur and Shah Abbas might be brothers. Centuries separated them, but it is their likeness to one another that we remember. Perhaps it could hardly be otherwise. Persia lay at the crossroads between the East and the West, and at the same time the country was almost inaccessible with its huge deserts and barricades of mountains. An invading army does not enter such a country lightly. Those who invaded Persia brought suppleness and strength, and the Persians themselves had to acquire suppleness and strength to resist them. Being conquerors themselves, they became a hardy, earthy people, devoted to their land and their memories of conquest, delighting in the world around them, cultivating the arts, generous in conversation, living as much in the past as in the present, and always dreaming the same dreams—those dreams that wore the colors of human majesty, so that

THE LAND AND THE PEOPLE

every Persian saw himself in some way as a King. Thus they brought into being Kings who were very much like themselves, but touched with a more fiery light than that which shone on their own faces.

One tries in vain to describe the translucent colors of the light in Persia, at once soft and glinting, gentle and fierce, motionless and in motion. There are days when the Persian sky is like a great beaker of blue wine, and other days when the wine seems to be poured from one side of the sky to the other. Most of all the sky resembles a blue flame, of a richer and deeper color than the flame which sheds its light over the south of France. It is almost as difficult to describe the strange, rich shapes of the Persian mountains— the tawny lion-headed mountains of the south and the immense snowcapped mountains of the Elburz, where the foothills are all the colors of the rainbow. If you drive from Teheran towards the Chalus Pass which takes you to the Caspian, you see mountains that appear to have been upended, tilted fantastically against the sky, in layers of emerald green and ruby red and pure white. A stream runs between the mountains, where clumps of willows nestle and fishermen stand on the banks. Here and there you come upon gardens with tiled pavements and long avenues of poplars. A sky like wine, and a landscape like one in a fairy tale. And the patient traveller, wandering through Persia, looking on glittering blue-tiled mosques and city gates covered with many-colored faïence, must often ask himself whether he is dreaming.

THE SPLENDOR OF PERSIA

Majesty! Fairyland! The blaze of noon, and the splendor of the blue skies, and then the splendor of the people who walk in that ancient land as though they expected nothing to change, for indeed so little has changed about them for centuries. Yet change is in the air. Slowly and surely Persia is being brought into the modern community of nations. Industrialization goes on apace, and a visitor to Abadan looking at the oil-refineries could hardly share the excitement of the visitor looking at the golden dome at Meshed or the brilliant blue and yellow tiles which gleam from the mosques of Isfahan. But even at Abadan you are aware of the sweeping softness of the skies and the proximity of the desert. In Persia fairyland lies always very close to the stern reality of the desert. Heaven and Hell lie side by side.

Above Teheran stands the snow mountain known as Demavand. It has the shape of a great shoulder lifted against the sky. This rugged cone of an extinct volcano has none of the feminine gentleness of Fujiyama, though like Fujiyama it serves as the symbol of the people who live at its feet. When you leave Persia, Demavand is the thing you remember most: a thing that seems to live and breathe, having a life of its own, powerful, flashing fiercely in the sunlight, veined and ribbed with immense stone muscles, gazing impassively on the endless deserts, standing like a proud sentinel against the sky. This mountain, rising so abruptly and unexpectedly above the Elburz range, prodigiously calm, scintillating, and majestic, is the sym-

THE LAND AND THE PEOPLE

bol of Persia. If you look on it, you can understand why the Persians for century upon century have regarded it as the abode of the gods. You can understand too their age-long reverence for majesty, for clean and shining and towering things. All through their history, on the palace of Xerxes and even in their mosques and on their carpets, you find them employing the symbol of the holy mountain. It is as though they measured themselves by that high pinnacle which takes on, as evening descends, the appearance of a living face—the face of a god or of a King.

THE SPLENDOR OF PERSIA

The Great Kings

Even today, though the archeologists have been at work for a hundred years, we do not know where the Persians came from or how they brought about the beginnings of their empire. All we know of them is that about 1400 B.C., when Mycenae and Troy and Cnossus were falling to the Greeks, a small army of

THE SPLENDOR OF PERSIA

tribesmen emerged out of the great plains north of the Black Sea and the Caspian and made their way by slow stages towards the Persian Gulf. We know that they came with horses and short stabbing swords and lances, and that they were an Aryan people with long heads, high foreheads and thin noses, and their blood may have already been mixed with a slight Mongol strain. They were brothers of the Scythians and the Medes, who also emerged from the great grasslands. Yet the tribesmen who were later to be called Persians—the Assyrians knew them as the *Parsua*—seem to have been of finer build than the Medes or the Scythians, slighter, hardier, and more warlike. At the beginning they can have numbered only a few hundreds. In time they were to conquer all the known world: Greece, Egypt, all of Asia Minor, all that was contained in the Assyrian empire, much of southern Russia and Afghanistan and northern India were to fall under their sway.

We shall never know the names of the first Persians who set the tribesmen on the path of kingship. They had no writing and no arts except pottery-making and no records have come down to us except obscure phrases in Assyrian inscriptions which may or may not refer to them. For a while we catch glimpses of them occupying the lands to the west and south of Lake Urmiya. Here they seem to have carved out a small principality for themselves, and the records of the reign of the Assyrian King Shamsi-Adad (823-810 B.C.) speak of a sudden raid against them and the

destruction of 1,200 of their cities, which may mean
no more than the destruction of fortified huts. A little
later we find them forcing their way through the Zagros Mountains and settling on the southern slopes,
living in the shadow of the mountains. By this time
they have become hardy warriors, and cylinder seals
show them riding to battle with gay plumes in their
helmets, the heads and breasts of their horses adorned
with jewels. We find them living in primitive wooden
huts, looking after their horses, watching over their
flocks, tilling their fields and sacrificing to their gods.
Occasionally we find them living in magnificent stone-
walled, many-towered buildings. Like nearly all the
other tribes in this area they seem to have worshipped a
Divine Mother who wore on her breast the badge of
the Sun and they reverenced the ibex whose curved
horns were sacred to the moon.

They were a frontier people, living on the edge of
the desert, with memories of having passed through the
forbidding territories of the Kings of Elam, who ruled
from Susa. They were good hunters and excellent warriors, proud of their independence; having no culture
of their own, they were beginning to borrow from
Assyria and Elam and the neighboring Kingdom of
Urartu and even perhaps from the Egyptians through
traders. Herodotus says they had no luxuries. They
despised comfort, unlike the Medes who lived in the
northeast and were closely related to them in race.
Already the Medes had acquired a written language
and were compiling the great code of laws which the

THE GREAT KINGS

Persians were to take over. Meanwhile the Persians were living strenuously in their fortified huts or in castles which were usually built on high plateaux. The princes who ruled them possessed absolute power; there were no slaves; every man had his appointed place in the community. They give the impression of people deliberately and quietly training themselves for conquest.

The opportunity came in 596 B.C., when the Kingdom of Elam was destroyed by an invading army of Assyrians. Susa was plundered and razed to the ground, the royal sepulchres were desecrated and the images of their gods were carried away. Ezekiel tells the story: "There is Elam and all her multitude round about her grave, all of them slain, fallen by the sword, which are gone down uncircumcised into the nether parts of the earth, which caused their terror in the land of the living; yet have they borne their shame with them that go down to the pit." (Ezek. 32:24) The great empire of Elam vanished from the map, and into this vacuum, when the Assyrian armies withdrew, the sturdy Persians marched with their prince Teispes (675-640) at their head. They captured Anshan, once a stronghold of Elam, and Teispes began to call himself "King of the City of Anshan." It was the first of the Persian victories: there were to be many others.

It seems that Achaemenes, the father of Teispes, had prepared the ground and was chiefly responsible for training a hard-hitting force of cavalry, since forever afterwards the Persians regarded Achaemenes with a

THE SPLENDOR OF PERSIA

respect bordering on the reverence they paid to their gods. But they rarely spoke of his achievements. The man who gave his name to the royal line of Achaemenian Kings vanishes in the mist of history, and all we know of Teispes is that he extended the Kingdom and at his death divided it into two parts, giving the northern part to his son Ariaramnes and the southern part to his son Cyrus. Ariaramnes called himself "great King, King of Kings, King of the land of Parsa." Cyrus, more modest, or perhaps less powerful, contented himself with the title "great King of Parsumash." Within a few years Ariaramnes vanishes from the scene, but not before he had caused to be written in an ancient cuneiform script on a gold tablet which still survives the proudest of all the boasts uttered by the Persian Kings. Remembering that the hardy Persians had depended upon their horses for victory, he wrote:

THE LAND OF THE PERSIANS, WHICH I POSSESS, HAS BEEN GRANTED UNTO ME BY THE GREAT GOD AHURA-MAZDA. MY LAND IS FILLED WITH FINE HORSES AND GOOD MEN, AND I AM THE KING OF THIS LAND.

Ariaramnes was the first to call himself "King of Kings," a title which Persian sovereigns have continued to employ until the present day, but we do not know how he lost his kingdom to his brother. For a few brief years Cyrus rules over Parsumash, Anshan, and Parsa. He is followed by his son Cambyses, who married into the royal family of Media. From the union between

THE GREAT KINGS

the gentle King Cambyses and Princess Mandane was born a son called Kurush, whom we know as Cyrus the Great.

At great length and in enormous detail Herodotus and Xenophon have depicted the birth, the upbringing, and the military conquests of Cyrus, who captured Sardis and Babylon and ended for a thousand years the rule of the Semites in Western Asia. His childhood games, his table manners, how he walked and how he addressed his soldiers—all these are recorded for us. He is the first Persian to be presented to us in three dimensions. We know that he was so handsome that long after his death Persian sculptors continued to model his features because they represented an ideal of physical beauty. He was tall and slender, with a straight nose, a firm chin, and thick lips. He had high coloring and walked a little stiffly, and was much given to laughter. He took his kingly duties seriously, but he was perfectly capable of being informal with his soldiers. He was merciful and deeply religious, but sometimes his enormous eyes flashed with anger and then the rage of kingship would descend upon him. At such moments he would drive himself and his armies into dangerous campaigns which swept him halfway across Asia, to die at last fighting some obscure tribesmen who, though a potential threat, were not worth conquering. Like Alexander he carved out a great empire, and like Alexander he did not live to organize it.

Herodotus, who often tells the truth when he seems to be telling extravagant stories, records that as the consequence of a dream interpreted to mean that the boy would command all Asia, his Median grandfather ordered him to be killed at birth. The herdsman Mithradates received the boy and was about to put him in a box and leave him in the hills for the animals to eat when he learned that his own wife had just given birth to a stillborn baby. The dead baby was substituted for Cyrus, who grew up to become a handsome and impudent herdboy. One day, when he was ten, Cyrus was playing the game of "Kings" in the same village street where Mithradates kept his oxen. Cyrus was elected "King" by the village boys and immediately set about distributing tasks among his subjects. One boy he ordered to build a palace, another became his bodyguard, a third was his prime minister, and a fourth his herald. It happened that one of the village boys playing the game was the son of a distinguished Mede. He refused the commands of Cyrus, who ordered his arrest and decreed a punishment—a savage beating with whips. The boy escaped, ran to his father's house and complained about the behavior of the son of a herdsman. The boy's father complained to the King, who summoned Cyrus into his presence. "I did what I had to do," Cyrus said, "and if you are going to punish me, I am ready for it!" The King was troubled. He recognized that no son of a herdsman would dare to speak in this way, and he saw that the boy bore an extraordinary resemblance to himself. He asked for the herdsman to be brought before him. Soon the whole story came out, and then once again the King sum-

THE GREAT KINGS

moned his magicians and asked what should be done—
should the boy be kept at the Court, or killed, or
exiled? In the end it was decided that since the boy
had played the game of "Kings" and had therefore
enjoyed all the prerogatives of kingship, though in a
childish way, he presented no danger. He had been
"King," and would be King no more. So he was simply
exiled to his father's Court in Persia. On the way he
learned the full story of how he had nearly been killed
at birth, and for the first time there came to him a
thirst for revenge against his grandfather, the King of
the Medes. A few years later, when he became King
of Persia, he hurled his army at the Medes and conquered them. Once he received their surrender, he
showed mercy. He spared the capital, Ecbatana. He
spared his grandfather, only making him a prisoner.
He retained the Median officials in their posts, and
combined the Median army with his own. Media had
grown until it reached out towards the Scythian tribes
in the north and included all the land touching on the
Black Sea north of the Babylonian empire. Assyria had
perished some sixty years before, and now there was
the Empire of the Medes and Persians stretching from
the Halys River in Asia Minor to the borders of India.
Two empires faced him—that of the Lydians in the
west, and that of Babylonia on his left flank. He
decided to attack the Lydians first.

In those days Lydia was at the height of her power.
All the Greek cities of Asia Minor paid tribute to the
King, Croesus. The Lydians had invented banking and

THE SPLENDOR OF PERSIA

almost possessed a monopoly of trade in the Eastern Mediterranean; wealth and treasure poured into the capital city of Sardis. Croesus seems to have been an able monarch with an affection for philosophers and no particular love for ostentation, though he is remembered for his wealth. Once when the Athenian lawgiver Solon came to visit him, Croesus asked him who was the happiest of men, and Solon answered that the happiest man he had known was an obscure Athenian called Tellus who had brought fine sons into the world and lived to see his grandchildren around his knees, only to die gloriously in a battle against the city of Eleusis and to receive a public funeral at the place where he died. "Until a man is dead," said Solon, "one should not use the word *happy*—it is better to use only the word *lucky*."

Croesus was unlucky. He had recognized very early the formidable power of Cyrus. He tried to awaken Egypt and Babylonia to the common menace and succeeded in procuring an alliance between them against Persia. Before the armies could move, Cyrus was marching against Asia Minor. The first battle, near the Halys, was indecisive. Winter was approaching. Croesus assumed that Cyrus would withdraw his forces and returned leisurely to Sardis, then believed to be an impregnable fortress, guarded by the best equipped soldiers in all Asia. The Lydians were excellent cavalrymen; so were the Persians. But Cyrus possessed camels and decided to throw them into the battle for Sardis, believing that the presence of the camels

THE GREAT KINGS

would frighten the enemy's horses, for everyone knows that horses are instinctively afraid of camels. The ruse succeeded. Croesus's horses turned and fled, but the Lydians hurled themselves off their horses and fought on foot. They were brave, but no match for the Persians, who sent them fleeing behind the high, stern walls of the city. Then the city was besieged. For fourteen days it held out. At last the walls were breached, and the Persians poured through. Cyrus decided to place the captured Croesus and fourteen youths from the Court of Lydia on a funeral pyre as an offering to the god Ahuramazda. Croesus stood very silent on the pyre, awaiting his fate, until he remembered the words of the Athenian lawgiver Solon, and then he was heard to sigh bitterly three times and to pronounce Solon's name. Let Herodotus continue the story:

> Cyrus heard the name and told his interpreters to ask who Solon was, and they came near and asked. But for a while Croesus kept silent; at last, however, when he was forced to speak, he said: "Solon was a man who ought to have talked with every King in the world, and I would have given a fortune to have had it so." Not understanding what he meant, the Persians again asked the question, and as they were urgent and gave him no peace, Croesus explained how Solon the Athenian had once come to Sardis and made light of all the splendour he saw there and how everything he said—though it applied to all men and especially to those who believe they are happy—had in his own case proved all too true.

THE SPLENDOR OF PERSIA

While Croesus was speaking, already the fire had
been lit and the flames were burning round the edges.
The interpreters told Cyrus what Croesus had said, and
the story touched him. He decided not to sacrifice him,
remembering that he was himself mortal and was burning
alive another man who had once enjoyed the felicity of
being King. The thought of this, and the fear of retribu-
tion, and the realization of the instability of human things,
made him change his mind, and so he ordered the fire to
be extinguished, and Croesus and the youths brought
down from the fire. But the fire had got a hold, and they
were unable to put out the flames. The Lydians say that
Croesus, when he saw their ineffectual efforts to put out
the flames, and knowing that Cyrus had changed his
mind, cried out to the god Apollo to remember whether
any of his gifts had been pleasing to the god, and if so, to
save him from his misery. Tears rolled down his cheeks
as he prayed to the god. And the Lydians go on to say
that up to this moment there had been clear skies, but
suddenly the clouds gathered and a storm broke and
there was such violent rain that the pyre was put out.

This was proof enough for Cyrus that Croesus was a
good man and a lover of the gods; so he brought him
down from the pyre and said: "Tell me, Croesus, who
was it who persuaded you to march against my country
and be my enemy rather than my friend?"

"My Lord," Croesus answered, "the luck was yours
and the misfortune my own. The god of the Greeks encouraged you to fight. Only a fool would choose war instead of peace—in peace sons bury their fathers, in war
fathers bury their sons. I believe it is heaven's will that
these things came to pass."

THE GREAT KINGS

So Croesus was pardoned, and Cyrus held him in high esteem, retaining him as a councillor in his court. Lydia had fallen; the empire of Cyrus extended to the shores of the Mediterranean; and the world shuddered.

The strength of Cyrus lay in his own character and in the character of the army he led. His soldiers were accustomed to privations, but they possessed an inner fire. "The Persians are proud, too proud—and they are poor," Croesus said once, unwittingly explaining the reasons which brought about his own defeat. Unlike the Lydians, they despised armor: they wore only leather breastplates. They lived simply, and were close to the earth. It had been hammered into them from their earliest childhood that they had only three tasks to perform well in life—to ride well, shoot straight, and speak the truth, by which it was meant that they should speak the true words of the prophet Zarathustra and worship the god Ahuramazda and the other gods. Half-enviously, Herodotus recounts the stern simplicity of their ceremonies; there were no flute-players, no garlands, no pouring of wine. Before worshipping, a Persian would simply stick a spray of myrtle leaves in his headdress. For a few more years this spartan simplicity remained; then, as more plunder fell into their hands, the Persians learned to enjoy magnificence.

It could hardly have been otherwise. With all the treasure of Lydia in his hands, and with the Lydian army marching under his own generals, Cyrus turned his attention to Babylonia, then ruled by the scholarly King Nabonidus, whose chief interest seems to have been antiquarian research. Cyrus was in a mood for conquest. He was also exalted by his successes in Lydia, and when he reached the river Gyndes and one of his sacred white horses entered the water and attempted to swim across and was drowned, he showed for the first time that sullen, determined rage which overcame him often in later years. He decided to make war on the river, saying that for daring to kill his beautiful high-spirited horse he would reduce the river to a stream in which a woman might enter without wetting her knees. He held up the march against Babylon, divided his army into two parts, marked out on each side of the river a hundred and eighty channels running off from it in various directions, and ordered the men to set to work and dig. The river squandered its force in three hundred and sixty channels, and having defeated the river, Cyrus marched on to Babylon.

At that time Babylon was the most splendid city in Asia. It lay in a wide plain, in the form of a square with sides nearly fourteen miles long, with the Euphrates flowing through the city. So says Herodotus, and we have no reason to disbelieve his estimate of those huge walls, which probably formed the outer defences. To enter the town, Cyrus once again employed the ruse of draining the river, diverting it into the marshlands until it reached no higher than a man's thigh. He chose a night when the Babylonians were

THE GREAT KINGS

celebrating a festival, dancing and carousing in the streets, and sent his armies along the river bed. Someone had suggested they might be entering a trap; there might be archers on the roof-tops. "If they climb on the roofs," Cyrus answered, "we have a god to help us —the god of Fire! Remember, their doors are made of palm-wood varnished with bitumen, and highly inflammable! You have only to set a pine torch to them, and then they will all run to their houses and be burned to death!" Then there was fighting in the streets, with the Persian cavalry racing down the long straight roads of Babylon and throwing flaming brands into the houses, and when the sun rose, the citadel surrendered. Characteristically, Cyrus ordered that the bodies of the dead should be delivered to their relatives for burial and kept the king a prisoner. In his proclamations Cyrus announced that Marduk, the great god of Babylonia, had thoroughly approved of the expedition. Allowing himself only a slight exaggeration, Cyrus caused an inscription to be carved on the walls of Babylon:

> Marduk bade me enter Babylon, going as a friend by his side, without a struggle or combat allowing me to enter my city of Babylon. All the people of Babylon, all the people of Sumer and Akkad, the great men and the governors of the cities bow before me, kiss my feet, are delighted with my majesty, their faces glow.

With the fall of Babylon, Cyrus completed his conquest of Western Asia. It was the end of the long

THE SPLENDOR OF PERSIA

story of Babylonian greatness, which Alexander the Great was to revive for a brief while before allowing it to crumble into the ruins we know today. For Cyrus and the Persians, Babylon was the turning-point. The petty prince of an almost unknown tribe had created in the space of a few short years an empire which stretched from the borders of Egypt and the Aegean to the deserts of central Asia.

To celebrate the victory Cyrus ordered a triumphal procession. For the first time he threw simplicity to the winds. He dressed his officers in Median costumes with purple, scarlet, crimson, and vermilion cloaks. He gave them padded shoes to strut in. And following the Babylonian custom he even encouraged them to paint their faces and put ointments in their eyes to make them shine better.

The procession, which wound out of the gates of the palace, was the most brilliant the Persians had ever seen. First came the bulls of sacrifice, followed by the sacred white horses. Then came two chariots draped with flowers—one dedicated to Ahuramazda, the other to the Sun. There was a third chariot with scarlet trappings decorating the horses. Next came the priests carrying the sacred flames. Finally came Cyrus in his chariot, wearing a blue tunic shot with white such as only Kings might wear, with trousers of scarlet and a cloak of purple. Round his tiara he wore a diadem, and he was accompanied by a charioteer who seemed puny in comparison with the tall King who rode by his side. With the chariot came four thousand lancers, behind it came the royal horses with their golden bridles and striped saddlecloths, followed by the Persian spearmen and then the cavalry and the tribesmen who had fought in his campaigns. According to Xenophon, the bulls and the sacred white horses were publicly sacrificed, and perhaps because it occurred to Cyrus that he was giving way to luxury, he decided to transform the place of sacrifice into a stadium where his soldiers could compete violently with one another. He himself ran horseback races with his Persians, and it is recorded that he won all the races he entered: which was not surprising, considering that he was "the King of Kings."

He was at the height of his glory. With the wealth that poured into his treasury he built two palaces—a winter palace at Susa, "Shushan the Palace" of the Bible, and a summer palace at Pasargadae, which means "the camp of the Persians." In summer Susa was so hot that even scorpions were said to die if they crossed the street in the midday glare. Susa, once devastated, regained its importance, for it was well situated on the great highroad between Persia and Mesopotamia and Asia Minor and on the trade route between the Persian Gulf and the teeming region around the Caspian Sea. Cyrus had one other reason for favoring the city: he believed that the waters of the river that flows past it possessed extraordinary medicinal value. He never travelled without a team of mule-carts filled with silver jars of this water. He also took the precaution of boiling it.

THE SPLENDOR OF PERSIA

After the great triumphal march in Babylon, he settled down to the enjoyment of his empire. He saw the dangers of luxury and did his best to combat them, but gave his officers the utmost licence, saying they deserved to do as they pleased and to adorn themselves in costly Median costumes and wear high-heeled shoes, so long as they continued to practice their military exercises strenuously. He made no attempt to invade Egypt. In the ten years that remained to him there were no revolts throughout his vast dominion. He showed an astonishing forbearance to his enemies and was notable for his zeal in making gifts. He allowed the Jews, whom Nebuchadnezzar had transported to Babylonia, to return to Palestine and declared according to the Jewish records that it was his divine mission to rebuild the Temple in Jerusalem. The Jews owed their new existence as a nation entirely to his magnanimity, and called him the "anointed of God." He was tolerant of all religions. He returned the gods which the Babylonians had carried off to their own shrines. He was one of those rare men who remain human when cloaked in majesty.

He died mysteriously—Herodotus says it was during a border-raid against the Massagatae who lived on the shores of the Caspian—and was buried at Pasargadae in a great limestone tomb raised on a platform above the ground. The tomb remains, empty of every vestige of its imperial owner. We know that the King was placed on a golden couch and wore his vestments and his tiara, but nearly two hundred years after his death, when Alexander the Great reached Pasargadae, he found the body lying on the floor of the tomb, plundered of all the royal ornaments. Such was the fate of the greatest of the Persian Kings, the man who was called "the Father of his people" by the Persians, and who called himself "the King of the world."

⚬✦⚬✦⚬✦⚬✦⚬✦⚬

CAMBYSES, his half-mad son, succeeded him. At the coronation at Pasargadae Cambyses received the tiara in the sanctuary of the goddess Anahita, and received a meal of figs and terebinths and a cup of sour milk in a solemn ceremony attended by the priests. Unworthy of his great father, he put to death his brother Smerdis. Determined to increase the bounds of his empire, he sought an opportunity to quarrel with the Pharaoh of Egypt, and four years after his accession led a vast army to the Nile. He captured Memphis and Heliopolis, though the citadels in both cities put up a stubborn resistance. Herodotus visited one of these battlefields some years later, when the dead Persians and Egyptians were still left lying on the ground. He reported one curious observation: the skulls of the dead Persians were so thin that the merest touch with a pebble would break them, but those of the Egyptians were so tough that they remained whole even when you hit them with a hard stone. Herodotus came to the queer conclusion that the Egyptian skulls were hard because they shaved their heads from childhood, while the Persian skulls were

THE SPLENDOR OF PERSIA

soft because they always wore their famous skull-caps of felt.

Cambyses raged through Egypt like a man who has gone berserk. Amasis, Pharaoh of Egypt, had died shortly before Cambyses entered the country. Because Amasis had defied him, Cambyses ordered the body of the dead King removed from its tomb. He ordered his executioners to lash it with whips, prick it, tear out the hair. The body had been embalmed and refused to fall to pieces. In despair, Cambyses ordered it to be burned, and went on to perform still more horrible enormities.

He scoffed at the Egyptian religion, destroyed the temples and with his own dagger stabbed to death the sacred bull revered as the god Apis by the Egyptians. This was only the beginning. He exhumed mummies, ordered all the Egyptian gods to be burned and opened the royal tombs in spite of the ancient curses laid upon those who ravished tombs. He murdered his wife, who was also his sister, by kicking her in the stomach when she was pregnant. On some trifling pretext he buried twelve noble Persians alive, head downwards—a form of punishment which was revived by a Shah of Persia in the nineteenth century. In a fit of anger he ordered his servants to kill Croesus, but soon afterwards he repented and asked that Croesus be brought to him. Cambyses was glad Croesus was alive, but furious with the servants who had failed to carry out his commands and so he had them put to death. Quite mad, he began to make plans for conquering the whole world. Only one great power remained on the Mediterranean—the empire of Carthage. He had conquered Phoenicia and ordered the Phoenicians to destroy Carthage, but they refused to use their fleet against people who were closely related to them by blood. Suddenly he was recalled to Persia by the news of a usurper giving orders in the name of his dead brother Smerdis.

In hot haste Cambyses marched to the Syrian town which had been called Ecbatana after the great Persian city of Ecbatana. There he learned that the usurper who called himself Smerdis was a member of the priestly cast, who bore an extraordinary physical similarity to Smerdis. Immediately on learning the news, Cambyses seems to have fallen into an epileptic fit in which he accidentally struck himself in the thigh with his sword. Gangrene set in. He died a few days later, after a reign of seven years and five months, leaving no children to regret his passing. His father was the greatest of Persian Kings, and he was the least.

With the death of Cambyses all Persia was in a state of revolutionary ferment. The false Smerdis ruled, but it was observed that he never left the capital and never called eminent Persians to private audiences. At first the Persian nobility were half-prepared to believe that the dead Smerdis had come to life again, but when seven young conspirators received incontrovertible proof that a usurper was on the throne, they acted quickly. The leader of the conspirators was the son of the Governor of Susa and a descendant of Ariaramnes, therefore of royal blood. His name in Persian was Darayavaush; we know him as Darius the Great. With the other conspirators he forced his way into the palace where the false Smerdis was hiding, cut off his head and showed it to the people. A few days later he ascended the throne.

The killing of the false Smerdis did not immediately restore peace to the country. There were Persians who declared for other forms of government than absolute monarchy. Together with the revolutionary ferment inside the country went a wave of protest abroad. States which had been conquered by Cyrus and Cambyses announced their independence. The governors of Egypt and Lydia refused submission. Darius had less claim to the throne than many Persians living at the time, but he had carried a lance in the last expedition of Cyrus and was commander of the Ten Thousand Immortals who had fought under Cambyses in Egypt: he was therefore a man to be reckoned with, and he set about maintaining his position with something of the strenuous energy which had been characteristic of Cyrus. For two years there were secessions and uprisings. Darius stamped them down. Babylon rebelled twice, Susa three times. The rebellions were mercilessly suppressed. Enraged by the behavior of the Babylonians, Darius had 3,000 of them crucified. But he succeeded in restoring peace, and to celebrate his victory, he had inscribed in the rock on the high cliffs above Behistun (the ancient Bagistana, meaning "the place of the gods") a solemn warning to all future rebels and

THE GREAT KINGS

usurpers. On the sheer rock 500 feet above the plain, along the old caravan road leading down to Babylon, Darius had himself depicted in majesty. His left hand grasping a bow, his right hand raised in salute to the god Ahuramazda who floats benignly above the scene, the King of Kings confronts his enemies—one prostrate usurper and ten captured chieftains who are shown with their hands tied behind their backs and a rope round their necks, in attitudes of supplication. In long inscriptions written in three languages Darius describes his own ancestry, his worship of Ahuramazda, his conquests, and the punishments he meted out to the rebels. "I seized Phraortes and led him forth, I cut off his nose and his ears and put out one eye, and later I hanged him on a cross in Ecbatana." Not one of the rebels escaped a similar punishment.

The magnificent sculpture on the cliff-face at Behistun remains to this day, hardly spoiled by time, the expressions on the faces of the King and the rebels still recognizable, though the rebels are deliberately made into caricatures. The long inscriptions, which were translated in 1835 by the young English soldier, Henry Rawlinson, after climbing the rocks and making astonishingly accurate copies of them at great personal risk, give the character of the man. They breathe fire and thunder. There is no pretence of humility. "The Lie made them rebellious: therefore Ahuramazda delivered them into my hands, and I did whatever I willed with them." But the next moment Darius remembers his debt to Ahuramazda and proclaims that

THE SPLENDOR OF PERSIA

the lands obey him only by command of Ahuramazda
and everything was done according to the wishes of
the supreme god of the Persians. Even in Babylonian
times the Kings had rarely identified themselves so
closely with their gods.

Though proud and perhaps corrupted by power,
Darius was in complete control of his own emotions
and there is no evidence that he ever gave way to the
madness that seized Cambyses. He was severely practical. He realized that the Persians were a small minor-
ity at the heart of a huge empire, and it was necessary
to pursue a statesmanlike policy. He allowed all the
nations in the empire to retain their own language,
religion, and institutions: the Greek cities of Asia
Minor were given democratic governments. He divided the empire into twenty to twenty-eight satrapies, depending upon the size of the empire at any
given time. The satraps were sometimes chosen from
among the ranks of the soldiers. They possessed the
powers of absolute governors, but they were watched
by resident commissioners responsible to the King
alone and in addition there were censors who travelled
continually around the empire, reporting any illegal
acts they saw and acting as "the ears of the King."
These censors possessed their own armed battalions
of guards and could inflict punishment at drum-head
court-martials. Though the satraps possessed vast powers, Darius imposed safeguards on their ambitions and
saw to it that they obeyed his orders at all times.

Within the bounds of the empire, save on the remote

THE GREAT KINGS

barbaric frontiers, there was peace—the peace of law. Having conquered most of the known world, Darius was determined to consolidate his strength. Vast tribute was demanded from the subject nations, but once the tribute was paid, Darius seems to have been determined to give them the utmost freedom. Handsome, energetic, a heavy man with a high forehead, a small upper lip, and a thick curling beard, Darius was determined to increase the wealth of the empire in every way, and therefore encouraged trade.

To help trade and maintain control of the empire he built a huge system of stone-paved roads which crossed and recrossed the length and breadth of the empire. The Royal Road from Sardis to Susa across Armenia was over 1,600 miles long. Every 15 miles or so there were royal inns and horse stations. According to Herodotus a man could travel from one end of the empire to the other in perfect safety. Imperial messengers and postmen riding along these roads by day and night brought news to the capital at fantastic speeds. Today, some of the main highways of Iraq and Persia follow these ancient roads, which pass close to curious mounds where ancient cities and towns lie buried, waiting for the excavators. From an airplane the traveller still sees lightly pencilled on the desert sands the straight lines of the roads which were abandoned long ago.

Though Darius wanted trade and security above all things, he was perfectly prepared to wage a war to safeguard his frontiers. He had always had a deep respect for the Scythians who lived on the western shores of the Black Sea. He determined to attack them. There were many reasons. These wild tribesmen, forever making forays into the outlying areas of his empire, represented a continual menace. They controlled the forests and wheatlands of Southern Russia. They also controlled the roads along which gold from the Urals and the Siberian mines was fed into the empire. He assembled an army of 700,000 men and led them across the Hellespont on a bridge of boats. Byzantium and all the Chersonese surrendered to him. A bridge was built across the Danube, and the Persian army passed over. But the Scythians remained elusive. They would attack the Persian forces suddenly, and then vanish. When Darius sent messengers demanding their surrender, they replied with impertinent messages. Once when Darius demanded bread and water from them—bread and water being signs of submission—he received instead a strange gift which consisted of a bird, a mouse, a frog, and five arrows. The King reasoned that the gift of five arrows meant that the Scythians were preparing to surrender their power to him, but one of his generals put another interpretation on the gift and said: "Unless we turn into birds and fly up into the air, or into mice and burrow into the ground, or into frogs and jump into the lakes, we shall never go home again, but stay here in this country, being shot at by Scythian arrows."

Scythia was hard fighting country, as the Germans learned to their cost during the last war. The ground

THE GREAT KINGS

became iron-hard in winter; there were blizzards and snow-storms; the Persians were unaccustomed to such bitter cold. Eighty thousand Persians perished during the campaign. But though the war against Scythia proved disappointing, Darius had made important gains. Macedonia and Thrace fell to his armies. He had put an end, or so he thought, to any possibility of revolt in the West.

In the year 510 B.C. two events of great importance to the history of the world occurred. In that year the Romans expelled the Etruscans from Latium and the Athenians expelled the tyrant Hippias, who immediately sailed to Asia and made common cause with the Persian King. Under its tyrant Athens had paid tribute to Persia. Now the tribute was suddenly withdrawn, and one by one the cities in Asia Minor began to feel the extraordinary exhilaration which comes with the desire for freedom. Miletus, which had seen the birth of Greek philosophy, revolted against Persian rule, sent an army against Sardis and received help from Athens. Darius ordered the destruction of Miletus. As for the Athenians, he ordered that every man should be made a slave.

It was easier said than done. The Athenians were in a mood for rebellion, and a small handful of superbly civilized men prepared to oppose the might of Persia. When a Persian fleet landed an army on the island of Euboea and attacked Eretria, burning the temples to the ground, destroying the city, and sending all the inhabitants in chains to Susa, the Athenians realized they would have to fight to the death.

On September 20, 490 B.C., the Persian fleet appeared off the coast of Attica and prepared to disembark troops on the plain of Marathon. They chose unwisely, for there were marshes on each side of them and high mountains facing them, and in one of the defiles of the mountains, the Athenian army under Miltiades was waiting. The disposition of the Persian troops was exactly what Miltiades was hoping for. He saw that the Persian centre was weak and ordered the Athenians to race down the slope, grapple with the Persians, and drive them into the sea. Shouting at the top of their voices, armed with spears or short stabbing swords, and with heavy bronze shields, the Greeks flung themselves at the whole length of the Persian line. Despair gave them courage. When the smoke of battle cleared, there were 6,400 dead Persians lying on the battlefield, while the rest fled to the ships. There were less than 200 Athenians dead; these were solemnly buried beneath a mound which remains to this day. "For the first time," said Herodotus, "it had happened that Greeks had dared to look upon Persians without flinching."

Athens had triumphed. A handful of men, whose names are unknown, had altered the course of history. Darius was enraged, but there was little he could do. The example of the Athenians was followed immediately by the Egyptians, who revolted. A few years

THE GREAT KINGS

later, preparing to punish both the Athenians and the Egyptians, Darius died, bequeathing his empire to his son Khshayarsha, who appears in the Bible under the name of Ahasuerus and whom we know as Xerxes.

The last years of Darius were a nightmare, but the middle years were peaceful. Never before or afterwards did the empire enjoy such prosperity. Under Darius it achieved its widest extent, and no other Persian Emperor showed such a gift for government. Before he died, he ordered that an inscription should be placed on his tomb. The inscription read: "I was a friend to my friends, no archer or horseman was better, and I excelled as a hunter: there was nothing I could not do." It was almost true.

❋⦿❋⦿❋⦿❋⦿❋

THERE WAS stern metal in Xerxes, but there was also softness. His features were milder than his father's. He was graceful, handsome, superbly aware of his powers. He combined a passionate love for beautiful things and a quiet intoxication with power. Once, when he was marching with his troops, he saw a plane tree so beautiful that he decorated it with gold ornaments and left one of the Immortals to guard it. If we can believe Herodotus, he wept when he watched his troops crossing the Hellespont, overwhelmed by the thought that in a hundred years' time none of the men crossing in the ships or crowding the shores would be alive. Moody, sensual, a man who

THE SPLENDOR OF PERSIA

laughed easily and sometimes gave himself to mean-
ingless acts of violence, he seems to have possessed
little real ability to rule and none of his father's me-
thodical devotion to duty. He was something of a play-
boy to the end.

He seems to have embarked upon the invasion of
Greece in a mood of profound apprehension mingled
with the delight of a man seeing himself at the head of
the greatest army the world had ever seen. He had no
illusions about Greek strength: he had been warned
by royal cousins and by Greek mercenaries that the
Greeks, with their backs against the wall, would fight
mercilessly and to the bitter end. Why then did he
command that ill-fated expedition? The reason is that
he had no alternative: because the Athenians had
rebelled, it was inevitable that he should make a supreme effort to crush them. Moreover, with three-
quarters of the known world under its sway, the Persian empire was compelled to attempt to bring about
a universal empire. That Darius contemplated a universal empire with himself at the head is clear from
the inscriptions at Behistun and in other places. That
Xerxes deliberately followed the path he had outlined
is suggested by words he spoke to his advisers shortly
before leading his vast army against Athens. "If we
succeed in destroying the Athenians," he said, "we
shall so extend the boundaries of Persia that it will
reach to the very skies of God! With your help then I
shall pass through Europe from one end to the other,

THE GREAT KINGS

and make it all into one country! Whatever the sun shines upon will be our land!" It was a proud boast, and might very well have come true.

In the spring of 480 B.C. Xerxes reached the Hellespont. There he prayed for victory, poured wine from a golden goblet into the sea, and afterwards flung a bowl and a short Persian sword into the sea as well. He seriously believed that he could march through Europe until he reached the Gates of Hercules at Gibraltar.

According to Herodotus the strange motley army which passed over into Europe under the banner of the Persian Emperor comprised 2,317,610 men, excluding army servants and those in charge of food transports. Herodotus added that he believed the total number of people who went over the bridge which joins Europe to Asia numbered perhaps five million, a number which modern scholarship is inclined to distrust. It is not however an impossible number. Xerxes was attempting nothing less than the colonization of Europe, and the war against Athens was only a minor incident in his campaign. Whole nations out of Asia were being hurled against Greece, the sole barrier against his ambitions. Consciously or unconsciously, Xerxes had put himself at the head of a vast and uncontrollable movement of expansion comparable with the great folk-wanderings of a previous age.

Xerxes was at the zenith of his power. Wearing the tiara and the diadem, and a gown of blue silk shot with white, he would sometimes slip away from his royal coach and drive in a closed carriage, invisible to his

THE SPLENDOR OF PERSIA

armies. While he rode down the coast, his fleet followed close to shore. The army and the fleet were so vast that he had difficulty in supplying them with food.

The story is told that when some spies were captured and then sentenced to death, they were reprieved by Xerxes, who commented: "Let them go back to their homes. They have seen the strength of our armies, and there is no harm in them reporting what they have seen when they reach home." Xerxes fought cannily and without hurry. He was waiting his time, determined to put an end to the intransigence of the Athenians. Even when he had crossed the Hellespont and the whole of the vast army had reached the shores of Europe, a healthy fear of Athens remained.

It is possible that Xerxes knew the risk he was running, for he seems to have been an inveterate gambler. His army had not been welded together, his soldiers coming from all parts of the empire. There were Ligyans, Mariandynians, Lycians, Caballians. Soldiers had come from places as distant as Ethiopia and India. The Ethiopians wore headdresses made of horses' scalps, the manes serving as crests. The Arabs wore cotton gowns. There were tribesmen who fought with lassos which they whirled above their heads, dropped over their enemies; then they dragged them along the ground and dispatched them with daggers. There were more primitive tribesmen who fought with wooden clubs sprinkled with nails. Most splendid of all were the Persian soldiers who wore fluted caps of felt, embroidered tunics, trousers and chain-mail, and

THE GREAT KINGS

were so liberally sprinkled with gold medallions, brooches, bracelets and little golden flowers knitted onto their tunics that they looked more like a river of gold than an army starting out on an arduous campaign. Officers brought their wives and servants with them in covered carriages. Xerxes himself, travelling in great panoply, seems to have regarded the expedition as a triumphal procession, riding immediately behind the sacred white horses and the empty chariot dedicated to Ahuramazda. Behind him rode the Immortals with gold pomegranates and apples instead of pikes on the butt-ends of their spears.

The Persian army drove slowly through Thessaly, and it was summer before they reached the Pass of Thermopylae ("The Hot Springs"). Here some 6,000 Spartans were waiting at the top of a pass, where there was an altar to Hercules and a crumbling wall, which they proceeded to rebuild. At its narrowest, the pass was a single waggon-track wide. The commander of this small force was the Spartan King, Leonidas, a man who was reckless of his own life and fortunes and determined to maintain the honor of Sparta. The Persians sent an army up the steep and craggy slopes, but were hurled back. Four days later Xerxes tried again. Once more the Persians were thrown back, and this time the enemy of the Greeks decided upon stern measures. At all costs Leonidas must be destroyed. With supreme contempt the Spartans had stripped for exercise and combed their long hair in full sight of the Persians. In revenge Xerxes hurled a huge force against

THE SPLENDOR OF PERSIA

them, even sending his private guard, the Immortals, into the battle. But in the confined space along the pass the Persians had no advantage from their numbers, and they were forced to fall back.

The end came when a traitor, Ephialtes, told the Persians about a secret goat-track which led over the hills to Thermopylae. Xerxes, who had been watching the battle from below, promptly gave orders for a detachment of his best troops to scale the mountains and follow the goat-track which would take them above the Spartan position. They marched under cover of darkness through oak forests on the slopes, the sound of their marching feet drowned by the sounds of the forest, then they fell upon the Spartan outposts. The battle was brief, the Spartans fighting recklessly, so many of their spears broken that they had to fight with their short stabbing swords. Nearly all died. Leonidas himself seems to have been killed early: there was a bitter struggle over his body, with the Greeks rescuing it from the enemy altogether four times. Those who lost their swords fought with their bare hands and their teeth. Soon the armies of Xerxes were sweeping through the pass at Thermopylae.

On that same day there was fighting at sea. The small Greek fleet edged its way close to the Persians, destroyed thirty Persian ships and hurried back to its base at Artemisium. During the night there was a terrible thunderstorm. Ships were tossed about like twigs. Wreckage piled up, fouling the oars. It was three days before the Persian fleet was able to sail to Artemisium,

THE GREAT KINGS

hoping to bottle up the Greeks in their harbor. They failed. Both fleets retired to lick their wounds. From Artemisium the Greeks sailed to Salamis. From Thermopylae the Persians made their way unhindered into Attica, and so to Athens.

When the Persians reached Athens they found it deserted except for a few temple servants who barricaded themselves in the Acropolis. They threw up wooden walls on the heights of the Acropolis, and the Persians simply shot flaming arrows at the wooden walls. The Greeks had the advantage of higher ground and rolled boulders down on the Persians below. For a while it seemed that the Acropolis, set on its rocky mountain, was impregnable, but the trick that was played at Thermopylae was played again—they heard of a secret path leading up the steep walls of the Acropolis, and they scrambled up it. All the defenders were massacred, the treasure was removed from the treasury and the Acropolis was put to the flames.

Xerxes had conquered Athens, but it was an empty victory. The Persians could go on and capture all Europe and see the defences going down one by one, but Xerxes had no heart to continue the adventure. He had overextended his line of communication. He seems to have decided already to return home when his fleet joined battle with the Greek fleet in the bay of Salamis. The Greeks were turning tail and giving the battle up for lost when they saw one of their ships being rammed by a Persian ship. Then they all swung round and went to its rescue. Emboldened by their success,

THE SPLENDOR OF PERSIA

the Greeks decided to remain and fight the battle out. They were good at ramming; the Persians were bad at it; and soon there were splintered Persian ships drifting helplessly across the battle-lines. The battle continued through the day. One after another the Persian ships fell to boarding parties of Greeks, and then when their sailors were hurled into the sea—the Greeks noted with pleasure that no Persians could swim—the ships were allowed to drift with the west wind towards the neighboring coast called Colias, where some years before a soothsayer had said: "The women of Colias shall cook their food with oars." Out of smashed oars the women made many cooking-fires. The dramatist Aeschylus, who was present at the battle, declared that he had never seen such havoc. There was blood everywhere, and the Greeks were en-joying themselves, hitting out with stumps of oars at the Persians helplessly floating in the water. "It was like smiting at tunnies," Aeschylus said. After the bat-tle the Greeks towed over to Salamis all the disabled ships which were lying adrift. They spent the night on the shore beside their beached ships, preparing to re-new the struggle. But when day dawned there was only the empty sea, with no Persian ships in sight.

Xerxes had won an empty victory at Athens; the Greeks won an empty victory at Salamis. They had destroyed a third of the Persian fleet, but the greater part remained, and the Persian army was intact, the conquered lands still in their hands. Had the Persians remained a few months longer, the history of Europe

THE GREAT KINGS

would have been very different. But Xerxes had seen his ships destroyed at Salamis and he knew that Greek successes might have the effect of stirring up rebellion on the frontiers of the empire: he decided to return to his capital at Susa, taking the greater part of the army with him, leaving only some picked troops under Mardonius, a capable general, who promised to deliver Greece into the King's hands.

Xerxes retreated at the head of his army through Thessaly, losing thousands of his men to hunger and disease. It took him forty-five days to march from Athens to Byzantium. "During the march," says Herodotus, "the troops lived off the land as best they could, eating grass when they could find no crops, stripping off the bark and leaves of trees and devouring them." Like locusts, they left nothing behind. Plague decimated them, and many had to be left behind. The bridges across the Hellespont had been destroyed in a storm, and so they crossed in ships. Food-trains were hurriedly assembled, and the soldiers who had been half-dying of hunger were suddenly feasted. Herodotus observed that these sudden feasts killed many who had been safe until that time.

Xerxes' invasion of Greece was an error of incalculable magnitude. The Persians regarded it simply as a punitive expedition, to be compared with perhaps twenty other punitive expeditions of which we know nothing, though it is certain that similar revolts were put down in northern India and among the tribes bor-

dering on the Caspian. The mistake was to under-
estimate Greek resilience. The Persians flaunted their
wealth and power as they marched through Greece:
this was another mistake, for the Greeks, instead of being awed, began to see themselves as the legitimate
successors of the Persians. The Greeks fought naked,
and laughed at the Persians going into battle, as Aristagoras said, "wearing trousers and having caps on
their heads." Also, the Greeks were perfectly prepared to change their tactics according to circum-
stances, and they had observed the rigidity of the Persian command. "They can be easily conquered,"
Aristagoras went on. "Few nations in the world have
so many possessions—gold, silver, bronze, embroidered
garments, beasts, and slaves. All this you may have for
yourselves, if you so desire!"

With his picked troops, Mardonius remained in
Greece for a year. He offered to negotiate with the
Athenians, who replied that they had sworn by the
gods burned in the Acropolis that they would continue
the fight. Mardonius, who was then in Thessaly, decided to seize Athens again. Once again they must be
punished! But when he arrived at the gates of Athens,
the Athenians were nowhere in sight—they had vanished. Mardonius set fire to everything that had not
been destroyed the previous year, and marched into
Boeotia. A Greek army timidly following at a distance
found itself, to its surprise, engaged in battle with the
Persians, and just as at Salamis they began to wage

THE GREAT KINGS

war hopelessly, only to discover that victory was falling into their hands, so they fought the Persians on land with astonishing success. Mardonius himself led his men in battle. He was killed, the Persians panicked and fled, and the Greeks won the day. The booty, consisting of gold couches and tents full of gold basins and bowls, cups and goblets, was more than the Greeks believed the Persians possessed. Stupendous wealth came to them, and by good fortune on that same day the Greek fleet burned the Persian fleet which had taken refuge at Mycale near Samos. Such a triumph might tempt the gods to think they suffered from the sin of pride, so the Greeks very sensibly offered to the gods a tenth of the gold treasure that had fallen to their hands. With the rest they prepared to strengthen the country. A coalition of Greek city-states had defeated the armed might of the greatest empire on earth.

Many years later, with the empire already in full decline, the historian Xenophon, when writing a Life of Cyrus, described why the empire had fallen into decay. Their crime was luxury. From being rude peasants, they became gourmets and sybarites. Once they had nothing but sheets and rugs for their beds: now they had carpets laid under the bedposts to prevent any jarring from the floor. In the hot summers it was not enough for them to stand under the shade of trees, but they must carry sunshades and servants would surround them with artificial screens. "Today they lay more rugs on the horses' backs than on their own beds," said Xenophon. "They no longer think about having a

THE SPLENDOR OF PERSIA

firm seat on the saddle: instead they think of soft cushions."

It was the beginning of the end. For nearly a hundred and fifty more years the Achaemenian empire founded by Cyrus remained, its power stretching from India to the Hellespont and beyond. But the great days were over. Between them Cyrus, Darius, and Xerxes saw the rise and fall of the empire. Suddenly it had arisen, and just as suddenly it was to go down to defeat. But before it disappeared, it was to leave an astonishing legacy to Europe. That legacy consisted of a particular way of looking at life, a sense of majesty and loyalty which had come to birth during the reigns of the three great Persian Kings. Underneath the gaudy surface, there was iron; and the Greeks who studied the Persians carefully were aware of Persian virtues and imperceptibly they assumed Persian characteristics. It could hardly be otherwise, when so many Greeks were living in Asia Minor and continued to acknowledge the sovereignty of the King of Kings. Greeks served in the Persian courts as artists and doctors, even as generals. When Xenophon decided to write an account of the ideal King, he chose Cyrus rather than any Athenian King. "Of all the powers in Asia," he wrote, "the kingdom of Cyrus showed itself to be the greatest and most glorious."

How great and glorious it was we shall never know, for the Achaemenian histories have not come down to us. But the modern traveller, standing amid the ruins of the great palace at Persepolis, can with ease

THE GREAT KINGS

guess at the greatness. There around him, untouched by the centuries, lightly carved into the immense stairways, are the portraits of the men who served in the Persian armies and offered tribute to the King of Kings.

THE SPLENDOR OF PERSIA

Persepolis, the Sacred City

At some time quite early in the reign of Darius a decision of incalculable importance was made. It was a decision which could be made by the King alone, for it concerned the capital of his empire. Cyrus had established his capital at Pasargadae, and there he was buried in an enormous tomb shaped like the wooden huts of his ancestors. Suddenly, for reasons that no one knows, Darius abandoned Pasargadae and made his capital thirty miles away at a place which came to be called Persepolis, "the city of the Persians." It was more than a complex of palaces; it was the cult city, the sacred heart of the empire.

We know that the change was deliberate and that until the end of the Achaemenian empire part of the royal treasury remained at Pasargadae, in the shadow of the tomb of Cyrus. We may speculate on the reasons for the change. It is just possible that the water supply at Pasargadae was not sufficient for the immense court which grew up around the Persian King: we know of at least one other royal city which was abandoned almost immediately after it was constructed for this reason. It is also possible that Darius simply desired to make a break with the past to signify that he came from another branch of the Achaemenids. All we know for certain is that quite suddenly Pasargadae sinks into obscurity, and on the spurs of the limestone hills which are now called Kuh-i-Rahmet ("the Mountain of Mercy"), beside a small river which flows across the Mervdasht Plain, there arose Persepolis. By general consent this complex of palaces and temples has been accounted the most beautiful the world has ever seen.

So much of the palace remains that we can reconstruct its most minute details. We know exactly where the King lived, and where he amused himself, and where he gave audiences; we even know where the drains were. We can walk up the great stairway, wide enough for five horses to ride abreast, and we can see the hundreds of figures carved in low relief beside the stairway exactly as Darius and Xerxes saw them, for time has dealt kindly with them and they look so fresh that they might have been carved yesterday. Massive winged bulls, derived from Assyria but given a characteristic Persian stateliness, still greet the traveller at the head of the stairway. The harem remains, so do many of the columns which supported the roofs of painted cedar wood, and so does the great stone platform built on the spur of the hills. Beside the doorways of the palaces there are carved figures of Darius striking down a mythological beast: though the palaces themselves have long since perished, these delicately carved figures are still on guard. At night, wandering among the ruins, it is possible to believe that Darius and Xerxes are actually present.

The splendor of Persepolis remains. It is even possible that it is more splendid today than it ever was when inhabited by Persian Kings for the same reason that the Acropolis is more splendid now than it ever was. Once Persepolis was a blaze of color. Embroidered curtains swayed between the pillars, which were decorated with gold and ivory. The curtains have gone: so has the gold and the ivory: and we are left with the bare and delicate framework, which is more pleasing to modern eyes than the overornamented palaces which once stood here. We know that the innumerable figures carved in low relief were painted in gorgeous colors be-

PERSEPOLIS, THE SACRED CITY

cause some coloring still clings to them, but as we see them today, the dark grey marble gleaming in the sunlight, the great processions moving imperceptibly towards the throne of the King of Kings, we are aware of a chaste outline and a delicacy of movement which is to be found nowhere else. Here is the first modern sculpture, the first brilliant awakening of the sculptor's art. The monolithic sculptures of Egypt were designed to express the majesty of the King and of the gods: they overpower us with their excessive weight and godlike dignity. Assyrian sculpture suffered from distorted perspectives and a curious distortion of the human frame, the muscles strained, the human figures seeming oppressed by destiny. But at Persepolis for the first time we see men going quietly about their affairs, conscious of their human pride. Here the human dignity of ordinary men was first expressed. From Persepolis it is but a step to the great frieze celebrating the Panatheneia which adorns the Parthenon, but this Greek frieze was carved a hundred years later.

The Panatheneia was a celebration in honor of the goddess who ruled over Athens. The carvings at Persepolis celebrated the god who ruled over the Persian Empire. These tribute-bearers and soldiers from the Imperial Guard are clearly attending a religious rite. They come in Spring, at the time of the Persian New Year, when the trees are putting on their leaves, bringing offerings which they will lay before the King, who in turn will lay them before the god Ahuramazda. They move quietly, perhaps to the sound of slow drumbeats

—the carvings are quite extraordinarily suggestive of slow and stately movement—and they hold themselves erect, showing no fear in the presence of the god. All bring gifts—humped bulls, camels, gold vessels, cups and goblets. They are all men, all are bearded and all show a grave maturity of expression—among these hundreds of figures there is not a single child, nor a single woman. One would expect to see musical instruments, but there are none. In the expressions of the tribute-bearers and of the Imperial Guards there is firmness, but not sternness: there is grace in the flowing draperies and gentleness in the depiction of animals. Zarathustra had insisted that men should be gentle with animals, and all the animals on the friezes are depicted lovingly, in great detail, and in a close relationship with the men who watch over them—the men always being shown *behind* the animals, as though it were the artist's intention to express man's dependence upon the dumb beasts. Here and there we come upon a servant resting his hand lightly on a bull's hump or throwing one arm over a horse's curving neck, and every gesture of the man conveys an astonishing depth of affection. The artists excelled themselves in their portraits of animals. Where the men at first glance seem often alike—though on closer inspection each is seen to possess his own characteristic gesture and expression—the animals are depicted with clearly defined identities. Yet the animals possess the same dignity as the men. The great frieze at Persepolis represents a civilization so powerful and so sure of itself that it must have

PERSEPOLIS, THE SACRED CITY

seemed inconceivable that it would ever come to an end.

The Persian histories, if they were ever written, are lost, and we must content ourselves with seeing the Achaemenian Kings through their own rare portraits and inscriptions and the accounts of the Greek historians. They depicted Darius as a man of firm temper and vast ambition, who gave way only occasionally to a talent for savage reprisals. Herodotus described a Darius who is immediately recognizable as the same King who is portrayed high up on the rock at Behistun. But Herodotus also suggested that Darius suffered from the corruption of power. The mute sculptures of Persepolis suggest the contrary. This long and triumphal procession suggests a people who were so accustomed to the exercise of power that it was neither a burden to them nor a cause for anxiety. All the twenty-eight nations subject to Darius are depicted, and there is not one man who shows the least sign of fear. Where Behistun celebrates the King's triumph in war, the frieze at Persepolis celebrates his triumphant peace. The wealth of all the world is being offered to the King, and to the god Ahuramazda who watches over the King's destiny, but as we look at the frieze we are never made aware of luxury. Instead we are aware of clarity, calm, maturity, the earth's plenty.

No other ancient empire has ever bequeathed to us such an insight into the characters, the costumes, and the appearances of the subject races. If the carvings were placed together in a single row, they would form a panel about 5 feet high and nearly 1,000 feet long.

THE SPLENDOR OF PERSIA

Here are representatives from a vast territory which extended from Ferghana in the north-east to Abyssinia in the south-west, from the Balkans in the north-west to the great plains of northern India. These tribute-bearers do not have the bearing of people who have been enslaved or who have submitted to overwhelming force: they are members of a commonwealth. The more one studies the frieze, the more unavoidable is the conclusion that it was conceived at a supreme moment in Persian history—a moment when there existed infinite trust between the King and his people. Such moments are rare; and it is to the lasting glory of the unknown sculptors of Persepolis that they were able to capture those evanescent moments and record them so powerfully, yet so humbly, on stone.

Persepolis was more than palaces and a great stairway. It was a place of pilgrimage, a temple raised in honor of the Persian Kings and of the god Ahuramazda. Here were performed the mysterious rites during which the King invoked the blessing of the god on the people. On the hills above Persepolis or among the foothills a few miles away, all the Achaemenian Kings except Cyrus were buried.

We know very little about the ceremonies which were performed at Persepolis. No Achaemenian books of ritual have survived. But we can guess the nature of the ceremonies from the carvings which decorate the ruined palace and from surviving fragments of the Zoroastrian scriptures. It would seem that in spring all the nations of the empire brought their offerings of

PERSEPOLIS, THE SACRED CITY

tribute; and while the priests offered up their sacrifices, the King of Kings offered up a still greater sacrifice—he committed the whole empire into the hands of the god Ahuramazda and received it back again. It is almost certain that the great ceremony commenced at dawn and that there was re-enacted the ritual slaying of the powers of darkness which is recorded on the carved portals, where the King is shown to be stabbing to death a huge mythological beast. Probably a lion was brought to the throne, and there stabbed, the blood being caught in golden beakers and then dashed over the parapet to fructify the plain. Then perhaps there were hymns to the awakened sun and the tribute-bearers would return to their homes with valuable gifts from the King. In Achaemenian times the King stands poised and motionless in the carvings, with a short stabbing sword in his left hand aimed at the belly of the beast. During the Sasanian dynasty, a thousand years later, he is depicted on horseback, his sword aimed at the lion's muzzle. In both dynasties the ceremonial slaying of the lion is depicted, but there are vast differences of attitude. For the Achaemenians power was something accepted solemnly and quietly, with a grave demeanour and an overwhelming sense of responsibility. The Sasanian Kings are nearly always shown on horseback, in violent movement, amid a swirl of draperies, and there is something in the tilt of their bodies and the expressions of their faces which suggests the calculated recklessness of powerful men. A new eagerness and impulsiveness appear, concealing

THE SPLENDOR OF PERSIA

an inner weakness. But in the time of Darius there was only a quiet assured strength, maturity, and vigor.

We shall never know exactly why the Achaemenian Empire fell into a decline. When Alexander the Great led a handful of men across the Hellespont and prepared to attack the most powerful Emperor on earth, the decay had already set in. There is no evidence to suggest that the rulers of Persia were unworthy of their inheritance. It is more likely that the empire simply died of old age and that the central authority grew weary of defending the immense frontiers. Bureaucracy ruled. Slowly and imperceptibly, after long periods of relative peace, the Persians were losing their cunning.

✦✧✦✧✦✧✦✧✦

THE YOUNG Alexander was confronted with a young King, Darius III Codomannus, whose yoke fell so lightly on the Greeks of Asia Minor that they took service in the Persian army and chose to be Persian subjects. The Greek provinces in Asia Minor were governed by Persian satraps, who took care to show themselves on their coins wearing Greek helmets and Greek accoutrements, and on the reverse of the coins there were usually typical Greek symbols. The empire was at peace. The young Darius III—he was almost the same age as Alexander—appears to have been popular. He was a tall, heavy-set man, dark-eyed and dark-bearded, and when he heard that Alexander had crossed the Dardanelles by boat and had captured

PERSEPOLIS, THE SACRED CITY

Troy, he seems not to have been unduly perturbed. He simply gave orders that Alexander should be seized and brought to the capital, and a small army was accordingly sent to apprehend him. This army consisted of Persian cavalry and Greek mercenaries, numbering about 40,000 men and comprising only a small part of the available forces under Persian command in Asia Minor. The two armies met at the river Granicus. It was spring. The river was in spate, with steep and slippery banks. Only an exceedingly reckless general would have ordered his troops across the river to face the Persian archers massed on the other side, but this is exactly what Alexander did. With a rain of arrows falling on his men, he forced the passage. There followed a long, confused battle. At one point Alexander nearly lost his life to the Persian general in command of the punitive expedition sent to arrest him. The Persian engaged in a hand to hand encounter with Alexander, and brought his sword down on Alexander's steel helmet, slicing off the horse-hair crest and grazing the skull. The Persian general however was killed before he could repeat the blow, and in the fighting that followed, the armored infantry of the Greeks punched a wide hole through the enemy lines. It was the beginning of the end. The enemy was forced to withdraw, the Greek mercenaries under Persian command taking to some hills behind the river, while the Persian cavalry fled. No attempt was made to pursue the cavalry. The mercenaries asked for quarter, which Alexander refused. He was determined to teach the

THE SPLENDOR OF PERSIA

Greeks in Asia Minor a lesson they would not forget, and he was angered by their resistance. He gave orders to his own troops to cut down the mercenaries to the last man. In the long, bloody, desperate, and fearful campaign which followed, Alexander showed little mercy to anyone. He ravaged Asia Minor, slew the entire population of fortress cities in Palestine, left a trail of blood wherever he passed. Bemused, the Persians watched the rise of a powerful force of nature, who obeyed none of the rules of war, despised diplomacy, and openly demanded that the whole Persian empire should surrender to his own small army, which numbered perhaps one hundredth of the forces under the command of the Persian King.

When Alexander set out for Asia, he claimed to represent the awakened fury of the Greeks descending in vengeance upon the Persians who had laid waste Athens nearly two hundred years before. When he reached Damascus, he found Spartan, Theban, and Athenian ambassadors who had come to treat with the Persian King, thus demonstrating how little real support he could expect to receive from the Greek mainland. The Spartans in particular, who were allied with Persia, regarded the invasion with distrust. And when after Granicus Alexander sent some of the spoils of victory to Athens, he ordered that they should be accompanied by the message: "Alexander, the son of Philip, and the Greeks except the Spartans, have won these from the barbarians who inhabit Asia."

The Asiatic barbarians however were in no mood to

PERSEPOLIS, THE SACRED CITY

tolerate Alexander's claims. At Granicus Alexander had had his horse killed under him and missed death by a hair-breadth, and from that day onward he seems to have believed he was invulnerable. Egypt was rebelling against Persian rule: consequently Egypt fell quickly into his hands. Even the loss of Egypt seems not to have disturbed Darius III so much as the loss of many members of his immediate family, who were trapped in Damascus. He offered vast ransoms, which Alexander nonchalantly refused. Darius III even offered to surrender to Alexander all Asia west of the Euphrates. This offer too Alexander rejected forthwith. It was written in the stars that the two armies would meet and decide the issue. The meeting took place at Gaugamela ("the place of the camel"), in the foothills of the Assyrian mountains. There had been a preliminary encounter at Issus near Tarsus in Cilicia before Alexander's advance upon Egypt, but though this had shown the supremacy of the Greek fighting power, it was not decisive and the Persians, caught in a trap, succeeded in disengaging their forces. The battle of Gaugamela decided the future of Asia.

The army under Darius III numbered more than a million men of all nations. The cavalry alone outnumbered Alexander's entire force. There were brigades of elephants and detachments of scythed chariots. The commander-in-chief was Darius himself, determined to lead his armies into battle like the great Achaemenian Kings who had gone before him, and in this, differing from his immediate predecessors on the throne. The

THE SPLENDOR OF PERSIA

Persian army with its back to the hills stretched out along the plain for perhaps four miles, outflanking the small, tightly knit forces of Alexander.

In everything that pertained to battle Alexander seemed to possess a sixth sense. A handsome stripling, curly-haired, his face remarkable for its beauty and the richness of its coloring, his head bending a little to the left, so that he always gave the appearance of someone who watches and listens attentively, Alexander entered battles as nonchalantly as he entertained his favorites. Told that the only hope of conquering the Persians lay in a sudden surprise attack by night, he answered: "I do not steal my victories." He slept well on the night before the battle. Then at dawn he went about the task of maneuvering his army with superb self-confidence. A sudden Persian attack on his baggage-trains threw the chief-of-staff, Parmenio, into a panic. Parmenio asked for hurried reinforcements, which Alexander refused, saying that it was altogether too late to worry about baggage-trains: if they won the battle, the vast treasure of Persia would fall into their hands, and if they lost, their own baggage-trains would be useless to them. Alexander went into battle wearing a gorget sparkling with jewels, a steel helmet polished to resemble silver, a tightly fitting Sicilian coat, and a kind of padded quilt which protected his chest. He carried a light sword and rode on Bucephalus, his favorite black horse, then growing old, so old indeed that at first he decided to ride on a much younger mount until the memory of Bucepha-

PERSEPOLIS, THE SACRED CITY

lus's prowess came back to him. Then he ordered that his old war-horse should be saddled. His army numbered some 7,000 cavalry and 40,000 foot soldiers. It was a bright, sunny October day in 331 B.C.

From the beginning Alexander took the initiative. To avoid the damage which could be inflicted by the scythed chariots, he arranged that his infantry should march forward in columns separated by the width of the chariots, with the result that the charioteers passed through the Greek ranks without inflicting any punishment on them and were later cut down at leisure. He attacked where Darius least expected to be attacked, in the centre, and having broken a path through the Persian and Scythian defenders, he attacked in the rear. From this penetration by shock the Persians never recovered. Darius took to flight, surrendering to Alexander all the treasure which had been concentrated some miles away at Arbela. The battle was won, and Alexander, at twenty-five, was Lord of the East.

When Alexander entered Babylon in triumph, flowers were thrown in his path and the satrap Mazaeus, who had fought bravely at Gaugamela, was reinstated as governor. Here Alexander rested his troops and consulted the oracles. Already it was observed that he was beginning to behave like an oriental emperor. His gestures, his expression, his way of addressing his troops were subtly changed. In time he was to take over all the panoply and all the grace and vindictiveness of an oriental monarch.

But first it was necessary to destroy all vestiges of

THE SPLENDOR OF PERSIA

resistance within the Persian empire. The enemy had regrouped, and was still powerful. Alexander marched on to Susa, the summer capital: it was undefended. But to reach Persepolis he would need to cross many mountain passes, where Persian armies were stationed in strategic positions, determined to save Persepolis which they regarded as a national shrine. Persepolis was one of the capitals of the empire, but it was also the place where the sacred Zoroastrian texts were kept. The tombs of the Achaemenian Kings were there: not far from Persepolis lay the tomb of Cyrus. Alexander knew the danger of getting lost in the mountains: there had been a time when he had led his armies backwards and forwards among the Taurus mountains, never certain whether the next valley would contain an army of Persian archers. Traitors indicated the passes which lay undefended. By a succession of surprise marches he forced the passes and attacked Persepolis when the defenders were expecting an attack from another direction altogether. He massacred the defenders, stripped the palace of the gold plates which decorated the columns, ordered the destruction of the sacred texts, sacked the treasury which contained 120,000 silver bars and 5,000 bars of gold, and held court sitting on the golden throne under a canopy of gold. Seeing him sitting there, Demaratus the Corinthian, an old campaigner who had been his father's close friend, wept, thinking of all the dead Macedonians and Greeks who were deprived of the joy of gazing upon his triumph.

PERSEPOLIS, THE SACRED CITY

For four months Alexander remained at Persepolis, carousing, drinking, surrendering to the luxury of the place and at the same time carefully planning his campaign against Darius. At a wild party just before his army set out for the north, he may have allowed a dancing-girl to set fire to the palace. Here is Plutarch's account of that strange conflagration:

When he was about to set forth from this place against Darius, he joined with his companions in a merry-making and drinking-bout, at which their inamoratas were present and joined in the debauch. The most celebrated of them was Thais, a girl from Attica. She was the paramour of Ptolemy, who afterwards became King of Egypt. As the license of the drinking bout progressed, she was carried so far, either by way of offering Alexander a graceful compliment, or of bantering him, as to express a sentiment which, while not unworthy of the spirit of her fatherland, was surely somewhat lofty for her own condition. For she said she was amply repaid for the toils of following the camp all over Asia that she could this day revel in mockery of the haughty palace of the Persians. But, she added, it would give her still greater pleasure if, to crown the celebration, she might burn the house of Xerxes who had once reduced Athens to ashes, and might with her own hand set the fire under the eyes of the King; so the saying might go forth among men that a little woman with Alexander took sorer vengeance on the Persians on behalf of Greece than all the great generals who fought by land and by sea.

Her words were received with such tumult of applause, and so earnestly seconded by the persuasions and

THE SPLENDOR OF PERSIA

zeal of the King's associates, that he was drawn into it himself, and leaping from his seat with a chaplet of flowers on his head and a lighted torch in one hand, led the way, while the rest followed him in a drunken rout, with bacchanalian cries, about the corridors of the palace. And when the rest of the Macedonians learned of it, they were delighted, and came running with torches in their hands; for they hoped the burning and destruction of the palace was an indication that his face was turned homeward, and that he had no design of tarrying among the Persians.

But if the Greeks hoped that Persia, once conquered, would be cast away and that Alexander would lead them back to Greece, they were terribly mistaken. Most of the Greeks who followed Alexander to Asia never saw Greece again. They rode north to Ecbatana, where Darius was believed to be; he had fled. They followed him across deserts and when they had found him lying dead in a mule-cart, murdered by one of his high officers, there was still no rest for them. The army went north into the snow-mountains and down into the humid plains of India. It was in a state of revolt when Alexander made his way back to Persia. Now more and more Alexander was in love with his faithful Persian soldiers, less rebellious then the Greeks. He made all his generals take Persian wives, and began to lead the life of a Persian King, wearing the long blue robe dotted with white which only the Achaemenian Kings and Princes were allowed to wear, wearing a Persian tiara, even speaking the Persian

PERSEPOLIS, THE SACRED CITY

tongue. He who had conquered Persia was in turn conquered by her. And at Opis he announced his desire to bring about a commonwealth comprising all the nations, a world-empire in which all men would be brothers, the Greeks and the Persians marching together as the heralds of the new dispensation. As an earnest of his intentions he married 10,000 Greek soldiers to Persian girls and presided over the ceremonies and feasts which lasted five days.

He was at the height of his glory, and was just thirty years old when he led his royal guard on a triumphal tour of Persia. The Macedonian Prince who had once ruled over only a few hundred square miles of unfertile, mountainous land had become the most powerful figure on earth. He made no effort to transform Persia closer to Greek models. His loyalty was not to Athens, but to Persia and in particular to the great Achaemenian Kings. He retained the division of the empire into satrapies, made the brother of the dead Darius one of his closest advisers and surrounded himself with the Persian nobility. He revived the Persian custom of prostration before the King and seems to have believed that he was divine and was convinced he was immortal. He planned to make Babylon the greatest city on earth. He prepared a great naval expedition against Arabia, and he was on the verge of putting into effect massive plans for consolidating the empire when he died after a two-day drinking feast, his last words (if they were accurately reported) being the harshest words he ever uttered, for he committed the

THE SPLENDOR OF PERSIA

empire into the hands of "the strongest." Some said he died of acute alcoholic poisoning; others of typhoid; it is possible that he died of exhaustion.

╪◎╪◎╪◎╪◎╪◎╪◎

WITH THE DEATH of Alexander, the empire fell into the possession of a half-wit and an unborn child. The half-wit was Alexander's brother Philip, the child was the fruit of Alexander's marriage with Roxana, a Princess of one of the northern mountain tribes. A regency was proclaimed, and there followed thirty years of confusion and intrigue, both Philip and the child dying mysteriously. The end of the fourth century B.C. found the empire divided. Ptolemy, one of Alexander's best generals, founded a Macedonian dynasty of Pharaohs in Egypt, while Seleucus, the most forthright of Alexander's Companions, ruled over Asia, and relatives of Alexander ruled over Macedonia. Seleucus inherited the largest share of the empire and established himself in Babylon, pacing the terraces where Nebuchadnezzar had asked long ago: "Is this not great Babylon which I have built by the might of my power and for the glory of my majesty?" Alexander had died in Babylon; the place was haunted; and soon Seleucus established a new capital near Opis. A little later, tiring of his new capital, he built another at Antioch.

Almost Seleucus was worthy of Alexander. He was a good soldier, an excellent town-planner and an admirable ruler. He continued the tradition of putting

PERSEPOLIS, THE SACRED CITY

Persians in high positions and married a Persian wife, Apamé. When he was past middle-age, he married a young wife called Stratonicé, whose beauty was proverbial. The King's half-Persian son, Antiochus, instantly fell in love with her. Love-sick, the boy pined away. The court physician was asked to report on the boy's health; and when the King was told that Antiochus was pining away for love of Stratonicé, he reasonably concluded that the best solution was to surrender her to his son, together with the western half of his empire. Afterwards, when rebuked for making so casual a gift of half an empire, he excused himself by an appeal to the divine right of Kings.

The virtues of Antiochus were those of a consolidator, his task being to preserve what Alexander had won, to fight against decay. He was continually travelling. He encouraged historians: it was during his reign that Berossus chronicled the Kings of Babylon and so revealed all that was known of Mesopotamian history until in more recent years the buried cuneiform tablets were deciphered. But the task he gave himself was beyond the strength of any man, even of an Alexander, and the history of the Seleucid dynasty is one of constant effort to shore up the ruins. Antiochus III, known as the Great, was compelled to invade Persia anew from his base in Antioch. He captured Sardis by a ruse and went on to capture Ecbatana, where he despoiled the last remaining temple, carrying off the golden columns and silver tiles which were famous throughout the world. It was at this moment that two distant forces,

THE SPLENDOR OF PERSIA

separated by vast distances, began to contend for the mastery of Persia—the Romans in the west and the Parthians in the east. Already the Parthians were establishing themselves in Khorusan. Roman ambassadors and Roman legions were already skirting the frontiers of Persia. And now at last the Seleucids, once so powerful and masterful, were breaking under the strain.

Partly it was the fault of the first emperor, Seleucus, who had chosen Antioch for his capital. That vast port, far from the centre of Persia, became a sybarite's paradise. Antioch-on-the-Orontes was at that time the largest and richest city in the world. There were long marble avenues and arcades, immense gardens, great houses with swimming pools on the slopes of the mountain which looked down upon the gleaming city: mosaics, colonnades, bath-houses, theatres. Nearby lay the Vale of Daphne, where according to the legend the nymph was pursued by Apollo and transformed into an oleander. This was the capital of Antiochus IV Epiphanes, meaning "the god made manifest." Antiochus IV adored the splendor of his position, and little else. He had a talent for buffoonery, turning his splendor upside down, as if to emphasize it. Once at the end of a feast he slipped away, and then wrapped himself in swaddling bands, so that he resembled a dead man. He was carried back into the festal chamber. A trumpet sounded. The swaddling bands fell away, and the emperor emerged stark naked, to dance a mad caper round the room. At another time someone shouted out

PERSEPOLIS, THE SACRED CITY

of a crowd: "You emperors are so lucky, always able to put your hands on perfumes and smelling so good." Antiochus ordered a flask of unguents to be poured over the man. Then everybody ran forward to smear themselves with the unguents, all shrieking with laughter, and the man who shrieked the loudest was the Emperor himself. Sometimes at midday, when he was drunk, the Emperor would ride through the streets, tossing huge quantities of coins out of his chariot. The heady air of Antioch had driven him nearly insane.

This strange Emperor, who submitted so supinely to Antiochene luxury, was an astute diplomat and succeeded in holding off the advances of the Parthians and the Romans. He was ruthless towards the subject states. It was during his reign that the Jews rose in revolt and under Judas Maccabaeus obtained the right to worship in their own way. But with him the power and glory of the Seleucids, the inheritors of Alexander's empire, came to an end. A few more Seleucid Emperors ruled, all from Antioch, all surrendering to the crushing luxury of the seaport, and all incompetent. The shadows of the Parthians and the Romans grew longer over Persia.

By this time Persepolis was almost forgotten. One of the great palaces had been burned by Thais and Alexander, and no attempt was made to restore it. Below the great parapet a fire temple was erected, and not far away there arose in time the city of Istakhr; but all the treasure, all the plates of silver and gold, all the costly carpets and silken hangings had been removed. Earth silted over it. Earthquakes and landslides cracked the walls of the tombs which had been carved in the mountains above the royal palace. Gradually Persepolis fell into decay, until men forgot that the world had been ruled from the great palace on the edge of the Mervdasht plain. In 1931 American excavators discovered the carved stairway, which tells us all we need to know about the might and power of the Achaemenian Kings. They also discovered the sealed boxes set in the foundation stones. Inside the sealed boxes lay small sheets of pure gold on which there had been etched in delicate Achaemenian script the words:

I AM XERXES THE GREAT KING, THE KING OF KINGS,
KING OF THE NATIONS WITH THEIR MANY PEOPLES,
KING OF THE GREAT EARTH EVEN TO AFAR.

PERSEPOLIS, THE SACRED CITY

The Divine Radiance

THE AGE of the Great Kings was over, but the gods remained. Cyrus, Darius, Xerxes—all had worshipped the Lord of Wisdom, Ahuramazda, and taken their strength from him and ruled in his name. He was lord of the rivers and mountains and the furthest reaches of the earth: he was a god who revealed himself in

THE SPLENDOR OF PERSIA

every flame, but he was also the god who breathed life into the Persians, guarded their cattle, protected them from enemies, gave them nourishment and peace and fair children. He spoke sternly out of the thunder-cloud, and in a more gentle voice beside the running streams. He owed his position among men to the claims made for him by Zarathustra, the greatest of the prophets Persia has given to the world.

Zarathustra—the name means "with golden camels" —was the son of Pourashaspa ("with grey horses") and Dughdora ("she who has milked white cows.") The family name was Spitama, meaning "white." It was this young prophet who gave form and substance to the strenuous worship of the god Ahuramazda, proclaiming that he was above all other gods. A hundred years after Isaiah and a hundred years before Buddha, he brought into existence a monotheistic religion of extraordinary purity, possessing in the words of Albert Schweitzer "an astonishing affinity to Christianity."

We know very little about his early years. He seems to have been born into a family of the minor nobility, descended from a line which had produced former Persian kings. He is said to have laughed at his birth. Many legends are told about his early years; most of them are improbable. What seems certain is that he lived quietly and obscurely until about the age of thirty, when he received the first of the great visions which was to alter his life and eventually change the fabric of Persian worship. He was standing in the sunlight on the shores of a river when his soul was led in

THE DIVINE RADIANCE

holy trance into the presence of Ahuramazda. As he told of it afterwards, the doors of Heaven were opened to him, the archangels crowded around him, and he no longer observed his shadow on the ground. Ahuramazda, the Beneficent and Shining One, demanded that he spend his life teaching the Persians the mystery of the one god. Between the ages of thirty and forty Zarathustra beheld the vision altogether seven times. He became a wanderer, travelling in remote places, living in caves and deserts, always alone and friendless, always attempting to make converts, and always failing, until at last he was received kindly in the court of Prince Vishtaspa in eastern Persia. According to one tradition he was over fifty before he made his first convert. Thereafter followers came thick and fast. The revelations of Zarathustra were brought to the attention of Cyrus, and soon all Persia had submitted to the one god. The religion announced by Zarathustra became the official state religion, the Persian King himself acting as the high priest of the mystery.

No credible portrait of Zarathustra has survived, but for centuries the Persians, and the Parsees after them, represented him as a man of prodigious dignity, very tall, with a long black flowing beard, his face shining with the fierce rays of glory. According to tradition he died at the age of seventy-seven while worshipping at a fire-altar at a time when armed hordes of Turanians were invading the country. At the moment when a Turanian soldier crept behind him and threw a tight

THE SPLENDOR OF PERSIA

rope round his neck, the thunder rolled, there was a
flash of fire and the body of the saintly prophet completely vanished.

Almost Zarathustra disappears under the weight of
the many legends told about him. It was said, for example, that at the time of his birth someone placed a
hand on the child's head, but the hand was immediately hurled back by the powerful pulsations rising
from the child's brain. It was said too that when wandering in the desert, he was accosted by the devil who
tempted him unsuccessfully. In revenge the devil slit
open his chest with a sword, filled his entrails with
lead and stood back to watch the prophet's discom-
fiture. But Zarathustra simply smiled at the devil, unharmed and uncomplaining, firm in his faith in the supreme goodness of Ahuramazda. We see Zarathustra a
little more clearly during the years he spent at the
court of Prince Vishtaspa. There are sharp quarrels,
feuds, attempts to murder him: he passes through all
these torments unscathed, continually intoning psalms
in praise of the One God, and sometimes the singing
voice gives place to calm instruction. He built up a
system of ethics. He warned, cajoled, threatened. He
spoke the words the Persians had been waiting to
hear. He asked that men should live together tenderly
and quietly and with true compassion for one another.
Above all they must live righteously, tell no lies, steal
no cattle, care for their dogs and worship the god
whose emblem is the divine radiance.

There is magnanimity in Zarathustra's vision of

THE DIVINE RADIANCE

the world, and some sternness. He had no patience
with the old Persian gods. He saw the world in simple, heroic colors—in the north lay the kingdom of
darkness and evil, in the south lay the blessed kingdoms of light; and men must defend the Light against
the encroaching Dark. By living lives of truthfulness,
by keeping the earth pure, by refusing to pollute the
waters, by shielding the sacred flames and by never
letting the air be defiled, men come to live in the blessing of Ahuramazda, and share the glory of the god.
Zarathustra believed in the power of evil. Evil threatened the world at each instant, and it was man's task
to put evil away, to destroy it utterly. He had no
doubt that good would prevail, but he demanded from
men the disciplined courage that would keep the flame
of righteousness burning. Then at the end of their lives,
having fixed their eyes steadfastly on the glory of
Ahuramazda, they would be taken to the Abode of
Song, there to live in everlasting light.

In its essence, then, the faith of Zarathustra was an
astonishingly simple one. There were almost no my-
thologies, no legendary stories about the god. Against
Ahuramazda stood the impure earthly spirit of Ahriman, the evil one, who contended for mastery, as the
night contends for mastery over the day. There were
priests, but their rituals appear to have been simple.
There were no temples except the small fire-temples,
where the sacred flame was kept burning. There were
no legions of gods, no archangels, no angels. Four
things, and only four, were holy, but how all-em-

THE SPLENDOR OF PERSIA

bracing they were! The four holy things were earth, air, fire, and water. It followed that men moved and had their being in a holy landscape, and it was enough if they dealt kindly with the earth and the rivers that watered their fields, the fires they worshipped and the air that bathed them. Seeing the world as a battleground between good and evil, Zarathustra established powerful supernatural sanctions for morality. The enemy was the Living Lie, and against this men were ordered to wage a war to the death. Every act of impiety, every untruth, every injustice, every pollution and desecration commanded its own punishment. He believed, as many Christians believe, that the eye of the Supreme Being watches men relentlessly and takes note of every fault. He believed further that men were born with free will, and it was within their choice to assist the march of the armies of the Good against the armies of the Evil.

Zarathustra's vision of purity had consequences which sometimes seem curious to our eyes. Because flames were sacred, no candle must be blown out, no burning log extinguished. Because the earth was sacred, no dead must be buried in it, and because fire was sacred, it was unthinkable that the dead should be cremated—they must be placed on high mountains and given over to the vultures. Because running water was sacred, it must never be polluted. If a man saw a dead animal floating in a stream, he must immediately jump in the water, remove the animal and arrange for special ceremonies of purification lest the stream fall into the

THE DIVINE RADIANCE

power of the Lie. Believing in the sanctity of earth, air, fire, and water, he was perfectly prepared to follow his beliefs to their logical conclusions.

At the centre of this worship stood the great figure of Ahuramazda. He was the Shining of the Heavens, the Lord of Life, the Giver of all Benefits, so vast and so powerful that he wore the stars as a scarf worn loosely round the shoulders. His body was composed of all the light and majesty of creation. According to Zarathustra, Ahuramazda's greatest achievement was the creation of man. "I created all things," he told Zarathustra in a vision. "Did I not create the stars, the moon, the sun, the red-burning fires, all dogs and birds, all the five kinds of animals: but better and greater than all these was the creation of the upright man." At the centre of Creation stood Man, and high above him stood Ahuramazda, the Lord of Brightness, the Supreme Power, to whom Zarathustra was forever singing hymns.

These hymns, known as the *Gathas*, form the surviving works of Zarathustra. We have no more than 900 lines of the words spoken by Zarathustra, and perhaps a fifth of these defy any kind of intelligible translation, but there remains enough to give the measure of the man. Here for example is Zarathustra celebrating the greatness of Ahuramazda by asking questions which contain their own answers:

This I ask Thee, tell me truly, O Lord:
Who at the Creation was the Father of Justice?

THE SPLENDOR OF PERSIA

Who appointed the paths of the Sun and the stars?
By whose power does the moon wax and wane?
This, and much else, O Lord, I desire to know!

This I ask Thee, tell me truly, O Lord:
Who from below upheld the earth and the firmament?
Who made the green things and the running streams?
Who yoked the thunder and lightning to the winds?
Who, O Lord, created the upright mind?

This, I ask Thee, tell me truly, O Lord:
Who was the artist who made Light and Darkness?
Who gave men sleep and waking?
Who gave the dawn, the noon and the night?
Who admonished the wise in their understanding?

This I ask Thee, tell me truly, O Lord:
Are all things as I have declared them to be?
Does devotion uphold the arm of justice?
Are good thoughts the foundation of your Kingdom?
For whom hast Thou fashioned kine as the source of
well-being?

This I ask Thee, tell me truly, O Lord:
Who fashioned devotion and consecrated her with power?
Who ordained that sons shall pay tribute to fathers?
Thus, O Lord, I strive to recognize Thee,
Who art the holy spirit, Creator of all things.

Devotion, purity, goodness—these are the words
that constantly recur through the *Gathas*. He asks for
no rewards unless they are deserved, and never prays
for abundance, only for what is proper to a man. When

THE DIVINE RADIANCE

he first stood in rapture before the glory of Ahuramazda, the message he received was astonishingly simple: "Let every worshipper show a divine obedience and reverence towards my Word, and so he shall attain to perfection and immortality." By the Word is meant something closely akin to the Christian Logos. It is never defined. But as we read these simple hymns we are aware of sublimity. Here is prayer unadorned, with a raw nakedness, and all the more compelling because it clothes itself in simplicity.

We shall never understand Zarathustra unless we remember that essentially he was a Persian from the highlands, a rugged man with a natural grace about him, not given overmuch to exaggeration. It was enough that the sun should shine, and the pasture-lands be fertile. A good man should have a camel, ten mares and a stallion, some cattle, a house, and if he has a wife and children and a dog to watch over his possessions he needs no more. As long as he fought the good fight, he could face the hosts of Evil with equanimity.

In time, and perhaps even while Zarathustra was still living, the doctrine became more complex. At first he spoke of the blinding glory of Ahuramazda, and from there he had gone on to speak of the abstract virtues streaming from the god's countenance: Truth, Empire, Purity, Piety, Immortality, Perfection, the Blaze of Light. Gradually these abstract virtues became identified as angels. The first of the angels was Sraosha, representing obedience to the divine law. His dwelling-place, according to the *Avestas* written

THE SPLENDOR OF PERSIA

long after the death of Zarathustra, was a palace supported by a thousand pillars which glowed with their
own light, the roof of the palace being spangled with
stars. Sraosha drove in a chariot drawn by four white
horses "swifter than the winds or the rain or the
winged birds." He wore the shape of an unconquerable
youth.

Mithra was another of the angels, and his history
was perhaps the oddest of all, for in earlier days he was
regarded as the greatest among the gods. Displaced
from his supreme position, he became the leader
among the angels, the captain of the hosts against Evil,
his place so high in the hierarchy that sometimes he
was invoked together with Ahuramazda. From him
comes life and increase; to him women prayed for
sons; he was the fatness of cattle and the piety of
priests. As Sraosha represented Truth, Mithra represented Empire. His single glance could hurl the spirits
of evil into distant corners. His spies incessantly reported to him the affairs of earth: he could decide at
his pleasure whether there would be peace or war between nations. In time the cult of Mithra was to shake
itself free of Zarathustraism entirely, and to extend
throughout the Roman Empire: there were temples to
Mithra even in London.

Together with Mithra, often standing very close to
him, was the goddess Anahita. She dwelt in the starry
heavens, and her function was to watch over creation
as the shepherd watches over his flock. She was the
protectress, the gentle goddess from whom there

THE DIVINE RADIANCE

flowed an ever-widening stream of blessings. She too had her chariot with four white shining horses. She was associated with rivers and all flowing things, and represented as a young and beautiful maiden, high-breasted and gold-sandaled, wearing a robe of pure gold and a cloak made of three hundred beaver skins. She wore only gold: necklaces, earrings, heavy bracelets. On her head there was a gold crown shining with a hundred stars. She was the vapor which rose from the water, the fountain flowing from the rock, the coolness which falls on a traveller when he comes out of burning sunlight and enters the shade. She was all that was dancing and gay. Though Zarathustra did not mention her in the *Gathas*, the Persian imagination demanded the image of the protecting goddess and she seems to have been the first among angelic creatures to have statues erected in her honor. In later Achaemenian times there were statues to her in all the big cities of Persia. Sheep, oxen, and stallions were sacrificed to her. She tempered the appalling majesty and power of Ahuramazda.

In the time of the Sasanians the books of Zarathustra were edited and vast commentaries were compiled, only to be destroyed by the Arabs when they invaded Persia. A small part was carried secretly away. Today in Yezd and Kerman and Bombay—the three places where there are still fire-worshippers who follow the precepts of Zarathustra—the ancient texts are still recited. But the importance of Zarathustra's teaching is not to be measured by the number of his living disci-

THE SPLENDOR OF PERSIA

ples. In all ages the Persian mind has been saturated with the peculiar morality derived from him. Long ago he became a part of the fabric of their imaginations, and they can no more escape from him than they can escape from themselves.

THE DIVINE RADIANCE

The Parthians

In 53 B.C., the same year that Julius Caesar invaded Britain, the Roman general Marcus Licinius Crassus invaded Persia. He was over sixty, and looked older than his age, a round-faced bullet-headed man who thirsted for wealth and fame, and seems never to have been satisfied with the wealth and fame he had acquired. He had already fought in many battles and shown himself to be a capable commander. He was already the wealthiest man in Rome, with a huge fortune founded upon money-lending and the control of the unscrupulous Roman fire-brigade, whose officers were not above setting fires and rescuing for their own profit whatever they could lay their hands on in the burning buildings. He was one of the three *triumviri,* who together ruled the Roman Empire. Power, money, women, enormous estates—all these were at his command. If he had been asked why he troubled to invade Persia, he would have answered that though he was a millionaire many times over, he wanted above everything else to lay his hands on the great treasures of gold known to be in Persia and he wanted also to return to Rome as a *triumphator,* a man who had subdued the enemy in battle, secured vast treasure and many prisoners, and was therefore entitled to take his place in the great ceremonial procession known as a Triumph.

All through the long summer of 54 B.C. Crassus prepared his plans for the invasion. After ravaging Mesopotamia, he wintered in Syria, plundering the temple in Jerusalem and securing his bases. Then, at the head of seven legions amounting to 35,000 foot soldiers and 4,000 highly trained cavalry, he marched into Persia. He believed the war would be over in a few weeks. It would provide an easy victory and yield a great booty, and he was not overly troubled by the thought that the Roman Senate had refused to grant him permission to carry on the war, for had not his

THE PARTHIANS

intelligence staff reported that the Persians were divided among themselves? Crassus saw himself as the new Alexander. He would dictate terms to the Persians, and for a while rule them as King. And sometimes, as he rode over the desert sands in all the panoply of a man who was at once a great political figure and the commander-in-chief of all the Roman forces in the East, it would occur to him that Persia was only part of the booty. He would go on to India, and even beyond, until all the East lay in his sway.

He was famous for his wealth, his elegance, his hot temper, his extraordinary energy. He was a master strategist in politics and a consummate organizer, but there is no evidence that he had ever studied oriental history. He knew little about the history of Persia. He did not realize that a Roman attack in force would put an end to all the tribal quarrels in the country. Nominally the Persians were being ruled by a succession of Parthian chieftains, who took care to claim descent from the Achaemenian Kings. They were men of heavy build, with broad faces, large chins, and bristling mustaches, and they had driven down from their camping grounds on the southeastern shores of the Caspian Sea. In time they had compelled the Persian princes to acknowledge them as overlords, but the empire they had carved out was constantly shifting in shape and the princes were continually acting as independent kings.

It was high summer when Crassus led his army across the Euphrates near the ancient city of Carshem-

THE SPLENDOR OF PERSIA

ish. He was in good heart. Near a place called Carrhae, several days' march beyond the Euphrates, he received reports that a small detachment of light Parthian cavalry was approaching. He summoned his generals, who suggested caution. It would be better, they said, to camp and rest beside the river Balisus, while sending off a reconnoitering party. Crassus was inclined to agree with his generals until his son, who thirsted for military glory, urged an immediate attack. The Roman legionaries were already weary of their long march across the desert sands, but the order for the attack was given. Almost at once the army was surrounded by wildly galloping mounted bowmen, who riddled the Romans with a continuous shower of arrows.

Surena, the commander of the Parthian forces, had studied Roman tactics and trained his cavalry well. He had calculated in advance the strategy Crassus would employ. He had drilled his troops until they knew exactly how to draw on the enemy, how to disperse, how to unite again. He had a nucleus of heavy cavalry, who wore steel armor and carried lances and swords, but he relied chiefly on his light cavalry, whose equipment consisted of nothing more than headstalls, a single rein for each horse, and for the rider, a tunic, a bow and a handful of arrows. The heavy cavalry wore chain mail which reached to their horses' knees: for the moment these remained in hiding in a small wood.

Crassus observed the light cavalry carefully and came to the conclusion that they would soon exhaust their arrows. When he saw them retiring after gallop-

THE PARTHIANS

ing wildly round his troops, he sighed with relief. But a few minutes later the light cavalry of the Parthians came wheeling back again, having replenished their supplies of arrows from enormous quivers carried by camels in the rear. Time was running out. He was losing too many of his men. It had become essential to punish these horse-archers, who knew exactly how to "leapfrog." Fresh troops were continually coming up. To make matters worse, the heavy cavalry, all glittering steel armor and pointed helmets, even the horses' heads covered with metallic lace, were now beginning to emerge from their hiding place in the wood. With a mixed body of 6,000 foot soldiers and cavalry, Crassus sent his son against the heavy cavalry commanded by Surena himself. Most of the Roman soldiers were picked troops from Gaul. Apparently disconcerted by the sudden advance of so many Gauls, Surena withdrew, continuing his withdrawal until the troops of the younger Crassus were out of touch with the main army. Surena pretended to be in full flight. Suddenly he gave the order for an enveloping movement. His heavy cavalry wheeled and presented the pursuers with a solid wall of bright metal. Against this wall the Romans broke, and the light cavalry cut down most of the survivors, taking only a few prisoners. The Gauls fought bravely to the end, and the younger Crassus, afraid of the dishonor which would come to him were he almost the sole survivor, persuaded his shield-bearer to kill him. With the death of the younger Crassus, the fate of the father was sealed.

THE SPLENDOR OF PERSIA

The Parthians were in no hurry. At nightfall Crassus retreated to the walls of Carrhae, where he sheltered his troops and prepared to march westward. There he remained during the whole of the next day. The next night he organized a retreat, but the retreat failed—thousands of horse-archers were buzzing round him like clouds of flies. At daybreak he made another sortie, reaching a hill he hoped to fortify and defend. It was too late. The Parthians charged them. Twenty thousand Romans were killed in a single day, and ten thousand were made prisoner. Among the dead was Crassus himself. His head (so Plutarch says) was cut off and taken to Armenia, where the Parthian "King of Kings" Orodes was attending a conference concerning a marriage treaty. The Parthians had been deeply impressed by Greek culture, called themselves Philhellenes and regarded themselves in some way as the successors of Alexander the Great. Orodes was attending a performance of Euripides' *Bacchae*. The severed head was brought to him, and he held it up at the moment when the actor spoke of another severed head, which is mentioned in the play. The Romans, remembering Crassus' ill-gotten wealth, liked to tell an apocryphal story of how he was found alive and molten gold was poured into his mouth, before his head was cut off. This curious story suggests that the Parthians possessed a sense of irony, which they showed at no other time.

The Parthian victory was complete. Only once before, at the battle of Cannae some one hundred and

THE PARTHIANS

fifty years earlier, were the Romans defeated so disastrously. The eagles of the Roman legionaries decorated a Parthian temple; the prisoners were taken to distant Merv and made to work as slaves. For the first time Rome had felt the full weight of Persian armor. Rome cried out for revenge.

When Julius Caesar returned to Rome, he spoke pointedly of the need to suppress the Parthian danger on the frontiers; and he was preparing an expedition to punish the Parthians when he was assassinated.

✦◈✦◈✦◈✦◈✦◈✦◈✦

ANTONY, the most beloved of the Romans, with his swelling forehead, his carefully combed beard and his compelling smile, was the next to attack the Parthians. Fresh from his conquest of Cleopatra, he seems to have been convinced that Persia could be taken easily. It was midsummer of 36 B.C. when he set out at the head of the greatest army that had ever been assembled against the Parthians. With him went 16 legions, 100,000 men, 10,000 cavalry from Spain and France, and some 30,000 troops from the Roman allies bordering on Persia. He had entered into a secret treaty with King Artavasdes of Armenia. Everything was in his favor. Orodes, the King of Parthia, had been murdered by his son, Phraates. All Persia seemed once again about to break apart into feudal principalities. Often in the past Antony had discussed with Caesar the battle plan for an invasion of Persia. Now he proceeded to put the plan into effect.

THE SPLENDOR OF PERSIA

At first everything went well. He struck into the heart of the province of Media Atropane, laying waste all the country. Elated with success, he moved so fast that he far outdistanced the baggage-waggons which contained his siege engines and battering rams. When he reached Phraata, the capital of Media, he thought he could take the city by storm, but it was well-defended. He raised a mound against the walls, this being the only way he could enter the city. It was a long, laborious task, and completely fruitless. Phraata resisted. Worse still, the Parthian King saw that the baggage-waggons were left behind and attacked the baggage-trains, taking prisoners, killing 10,000 men and breaking up all the engines which were being brought across the desert. From the walls of Phraata the Parthians taunted the Romans with their failure; and one by one the allies of the Romans slipped away.

Even then Antony refused to acknowledge defeat. His men were already suffering from lack of food. He decided to move away from Phraata with ten legions and three praetorian cohorts of heavy infantry, hoping to draw the clouds of Parthians who were assembling from all directions into battle. It was a suicidal maneuver. He marched his troops as though they were on parade, while the Parthians, who had gradually formed into a semicircle, watched in silence as the Romans advanced in long disciplined columns, rank after rank passing at exactly equal distances, every foot soldier holding his pike in exactly the same way, every officer stern and expressionless. They came in a

THE PARTHIANS

straight line, huge, mechanical, glittering. They held their standards high, and never looked to right or left, and resembled a vast army of jackbooted Prussians marching in strict formation. As for the Parthians, they resembled cowboys. Antony might have guessed that fighting cowboys have advantages sometimes over machinelike armies.

Suddenly, at a signal from Antony, the Roman cavalry wheeled sharply and raced against the Parthians, followed by the infantry which made such a noise as they screamed their war-cries and rattled their arms that the Parthian horses turned tail and fled. The Parthian horses were faster than the Roman ones, and when the battle was over, Antony counted only eighty Parthian dead. More significantly, there were only thirty prisoners. In despair Antony returned to Phraata, to discover that the troops he had left there had panicked and the great mound constructed so laboriously had been left unguarded. To punish them, Antony ordered that they should be decimated. One in ten of the Roman guard left behind at Phraata was executed.

The panic of the guards was soon communicated to the rest of the army. The machine liked to fight machines; it seemed not to know how to fight against mounted Parthian bowmen, who came out of the rolling grass-covered hills, made sudden thrusts, then melted. They were wise in guerrilla tactics, those Parthians who could spend three or four days on their horses without dismounting. They had a habit of com-

THE SPLENDOR OF PERSIA

ing up stealthily upon foraging parties. They refused to fight pitched battles, and continually exasperated the Romans with taunts. The Parthian King offered Antony a safe conduct through his territory, if only he would depart for Syria. Antony agreed to go, so ashamed that when the time came for him to speak to his troops, he asked someone else to speak for him instead. A Persian friendly to the Romans offered to lead the way to safety. Antony, distrusting him, put him in chains, but continually sought his advice; and it was this chained Persian who, seeing the banks of a river broken down, decided that the Parthians were waiting nearby in an ambush and warned Antony in time. Antony had taken the precaution of bringing with him a corps of slingers, who used lead bullets. With their help he forced his way through the ambush, but he was still far from Syria. For twenty-five more days the Romans staggered over rough mountains towards their base, starving, footsore, completely baffled and confused by the Parthians who plundered their tents, cut up foraging parties and hovered round them like vultures awaiting the moment when an animal expires.

It is one of the axioms of war that nothing is so difficult as to lead a retreat through hostile country. Antony gained no glory from his conduct in leading his men, and he seems to have known quite early that he was doomed to disaster. Once he threatened to appear before his troops wearing a mourning habit, and was only at the last moment dissuaded. When he addressed his soldiers, wearing a commander's scarlet

THE PARTHIANS

cloak, he begged heaven to visit punishment on himself alone, so long as his armies gained victories.

There were occasional successes, when the enraged lion raised a heavy paw and scattered the marauding Parthian raiders. More often there was stark failure. Famine had come. The Romans had to fight for their corn. Barley loaves were worth their weight in silver. The soldiers took to eating wild plants, which produced sickness and death. They went about carrying in their helmets their precious supplies of water they found during the retreat. There was one plant which sent men mad: soldiers who should have been defending themselves were seen moving great stones about for no reason at all except that it seemed to be a matter of immense consequence to them. "Through all the camp," relates Plutarch, "there was nothing to be seen but men grubbing upon the ground at stones, which they carried from place to place. In the end they threw up bile and died, and wine, which was thought to be an antidote to their mania, completely failed them." The soldiers quarrelled and killed each other for money; and they would have mutinied against Antony if they had not been so frightened by the presence of the hovering Parthians.

In the course of twenty-seven weary days the Romans fought eighteen battles and lost 20,000 foot-soldiers and 4,000 horsemen, and more than half of these perished from hunger and disease. At a place called White River, just north of Tabriz, the survivors of the retreat finally reached safety. A few days later, Queen

THE SPLENDOR OF PERSIA

Cleopatra joined them, bringing much-needed clothing and money for the troops. Phraates celebrated his victory by striking his own emblems on the coins of Antony and Cleopatra captured by the Parthians, which he found in the Roman baggage-trains. In the following year Antony, determined to avenge his honor, entered Persia again, but was no more successful in defeating a powerful enemy. Not long afterwards, having raised his son by Cleopatra to the dignity of King of Persia, though Persia was still unconquered, he killed himself when his fleet was destroyed by Octavian.

"A most peaceful people, the Persians," Cicero had said, before becoming governor of Cilicia. He was to learn later that they were rarely peaceful and were especially lacking in peaceful intentions when confronted with a Roman army. When Octavian became sole Emperor with the title of Augustus Caesar, many Romans believed the time had come for one last punitive expedition against Persia. "Who fears the Romans while Augustus lives?" asked the poet Horace. Augustus feared them, and took pains to keep the peace with them. The captured eagles of Crassus were returned to Rome, a sign that peace had been established. Then for a hundred years Rome and Persia lived peacefully together.

꜠꙰꜠꙰꜠꙰꜠꙰꜠꙰꜠

WHEN Trajan came to the throne in A.D. 98 there was a new spirit in the air. The empire

THE PARTHIANS

which Augustus Caesar had maintained so peacefully began to crack at the frontiers. Trajan revived the old imperial dreams of Crassus and Julius Caesar, who had hoped to see the Roman Empire extend to the Indian Ocean. He marched down the Euphrates and conquered Ctesiphon, the Parthian capital, where among his spoils was the daughter of the Parthian King and a golden throne. The Romans, fighting vigorously, avenged their defeats, but the Parthian armies were still as elusive as ever, and their fortresses (except Ctesiphon) remained impregnable. Trajan marched down to the Persian Gulf. He was sixty-five, and all his life he had been a soldier; and he was worn out by the long campaign in Persia. Looking towards India, he is supposed to have said: "If only I were younger." On his return march he attempted to reduce the great Parthian fortress at Hatra. It was a mistake. Summer was coming on. There was no food, there were flies everywhere, the drinking water was foul, and the Roman troops were weary of the campaign. Once again a great and powerful Roman army, attempting to reduce a fortress, was on the verge of mutiny. Trajan called off the attack and sadly led his armies away. Inexplicably Roman coins began to show the words: PARTHIA CAPTA. A few months later Trajan died, receiving the honor of a triumph after his death. There had been no victory.

Exactly eighty years later, in A.D. 197, the Emperor Septimius Severus, an African by birth, again led an army against Persia. Once again Hatra was attacked.

THE SPLENDOR OF PERSIA

The Parthian defenders poured burning naphtha and huge jars filled with scorpions down on the attackers. Fighting desperately, they held off the Romans for twenty days. Then Septimius Severus broke off the attack, afraid his troops would revolt, weary of the heat and the incessant taunts of the Parthians from behind the safe walls of their fortress.

The last Roman attack on Persia while it was governed by Parthian Kings followed soon after. For eight years the Roman Empire was ruled by Septimius Severus's mad son, Caracalla. More murderous even than Nero, Caracalla enjoyed ordering blood-baths and he particularly delighted in bringing them about unexpectedly. While living in Antioch, he decided to put an end to the rule of the Parthians. He suggested to the Persian envoys that if he married the daughter of the Parthian King, there would be peace between the two countries. He so charmed the envoys that they agreed immediately and suggested that the wedding should take place in Ctesiphon, the winter capital of the Parthian Kings. Caracalla accordingly journeyed to Ctesiphon with an armed escort, and when the populace was rejoicing in the marriage festival, he gave the signal to his soldiers to massacre all the Parthians they could.

Caracalla possessed a talent for massacre which improved with experience. Having murdered most of the Parthian Princes, he now decided to destroy the dead Princes who had once ruled over the land. So he rode to Arbela, where the Parthian royal tombs were kept,

THE PARTHIANS

and scattered the contents. The Parthians, though exhausted, swore vengeance, collected a huge army and were about to fall upon the Romans when Caracalla was murdered by Macrinus, the prefect of the guard, who had waited until they reached a place very suitable for murdering ambitious and dangerous Emperors —the place was Carrhae, where the army of Crassus had been torn to pieces.

The battle which ended the struggle between Rome and the Parthian Kings was fought between Macrinus, who acclaimed himself Emperor, and Artabanus IV, the last Parthian King. The battle was won by the Parthians. Of this battle the historian Herodian relates that "the corpses were piled so high that they impeded the movements of the troops and in the end the two sides could hardly see one another." Macrinus was forced to surrender all the treasure and all the prisoners captured by Caracalla. The remnant of his army was allowed to march to the west after he had paid a sum equivalent to three million dollars in compensation for the sacrilege of the tombs at Arbela.

But the days of the Parthian Kings were numbered. From the beginning they had been strangers in Persia, without roots, borrowing their culture from whatever sources lay at hand, so that their coins and their works of art were based upon Greek models, and their court rituals derived from the Achaemenians, and their architecture was a curious amalgam of Achaemenian, Assyrian, and Greek. For two and a half centuries these horsemen from the north dominated Persia and held off the

THE SPLENDOR OF PERSIA

encroachments of the Romans, but though they possessed an instinct for fighting, they seem to have possessed little instinct for government. The heavy, sad-
eyed faces of their Kings peer at us from their imperial
coins. A few are superbly handsome, and may have been
of pure Persian blood. They wear tiaras and crowns,
curl their beards, wear heavy necklaces, and have the air
of conquerors, graceless, impassive, a little perplexed.
Without them, Persia might never have emerged victorious from the long struggle with the formidable
Roman Empire; with them, the Persians were in danger
of losing their souls. And when at last they crumbled before the awakened consciousness of the Persian people,
they left behind so little trace of themselves that it was
almost as though they had never been. Of all the dynasties which have ruled over Persia, they were the least
successful in leaving a permanent mark on the people.

We know too little about the Parthians to be able to
make any final estimates. The Persians from the beginning have possessed a love for simple clear-cut lines,
bright flame-like colors, vivid imaginations: the little
Parthian art which has survived seems curiously subdued, complex, weighted with the heaviness of dread.
They had strange burial customs: the corpses were
placed in blue-glazed "slipper-coffins," into which they
were drawn by cords tied round the ankles. They were
brothers to their horses, those splendid "blood-sweat-
ing" horses, which were the envy of the Chinese, who
sent embassies to them and regarded them with almost
childish amazement. They called themselves Philhel-

THE PARTHIANS

lenes, and seem to have spoken Greek at court, and
their architecture is more Greek than Roman, but the
subtleties of the Greek spirit were foreign to them.
Philostratus the Athenian, a contemporary of Caracalla,
journeyed to the Parthian palace in Babylon and described it at some length:

> The palace is roofed with brass and a bright light
> flashes from it. It has chambers for women and for men,
> and porticoes which gleam with silver and cloth-of-gold
> embroideries, and there are slabs of solid gold let into the
> walls like pictures. The designs of the embroideries are
> taken from Greek mythology and include representa-
> tions of Andromeda and Orpheus. . . . One chamber
> for the men has a roof fashioned into a vault like the
> heavens composed entirely of sapphires, which are the
> bluest of stones and resemble the sky in color.

There is no reason why we should disbelieve Philostratus. Wealth poured into the treasuries of these conquerors: they were very likely to place thin slabs of
gold on the walls to demonstrate their wealth and
power. Philostratus also tells the story of four golden
magic wheels which hung above the King's jewelled
throne, designed to fall upon the King if he exalted himself above the human condition. The Parthians seem
to have worshipped the gods Ahuramazda, Mithra, and
Anahita, but without enthusiasm.

As we look back on the long reign of the Parthian
Kings, we are aware of the smoke of battle. Through
the smoke we observe sudden forays of armored cavalry,

THE SPLENDOR OF PERSIA

with their chain-mail and pointed helmets resembling Crusaders: the gleam of spears and javelins, sudden feints, terrifying mobility, a merciless and cunning race which had taken the measure of the Romans, and held the Persians in bondage. Only once does the smoke clear completely. At some period towards the end of their long rule, towards the end of the second century, an unknown artist made a full-length portrait of a Parthian prince in bronze. It is larger than life, huge and majestic. On the thick neck lies a head of astonishing power: the face of a commander at the moment of triumph, who is yet indifferent to his triumph, because he has known that it would come about. He stands foursquare, his trimmed mustaches swept back, his eyes wide-open, his chin jutting forward, wearing a short woollen coat of Chinese design and chaps of soft leather which have wrinkled into loose folds. He wears no adornments, and has no need of them. It is the face and posture of a man who knows exactly where he is going and will suffer nothing to stand in his path, stern, ruthless and implacable, without resilience and without too much intelligence. In that portrait is expressed all the triumph and the tragedy of the Parthians.

THE PARTHIANS

The Sasanians

IN THE province of Fars in South Persia the religion of Zarathustra lived on quietly. Here the priests attended to the sacred fires, and the poems of the prophet and fragments of ancient literature survived. The eternal war waged between the spirits of light and the spirits of darkness was quietly accepted in this province, where the rule of the Parthian Emperors was least effective. The rulers of the land were feudal princes, usually relatives of the Parthian Emperor, but the spiritual rulers were the high priests, who diligently served the gods Ahuramazda, Mithra, and Anahita, and saw that the injunctions of the prophet were rigorously observed—no corpses were to pollute the earth, no flames were to be blown out, the divine radiance must be worshipped, and all must pay appropriate penances for their sins. In all Persia there was no place where the ancient Zoroastrian rituals were so carefully observed as in the province of Fars, where the tombs of the Achaemenian Kings remained to remind believers of the splendor of their past. In Fars men dreamed of a time when a purely Persian dynasty would be on the throne.

During the early years of their rule the Parthians had despised the Zoroastrian faith. Now, as their hold on the people diminished, they began to make concessions to the faith which the Persians had secretly upheld since Achaemenian times. The Parthian King Vologases III ordered that the ancient Zoroastrian texts be carefully collected and preserved. When a ruthless sovereign begins to make concessions, the people, suddenly made aware of their power, begin to claim still greater concessions. So it happened then: there followed a vast upsurge of feeling for the ancient Persia which the Parthians thought they had stamped out of existence. The priests fanned the flames. A man living during the closing years of the Parthian Empire could almost have prophesied that rebellion would break out in Fars and

THE SASANIANS

that the leader of the rebellion would be a young Prince, perhaps belonging to a priestly family, claiming descent from the Achaemenian Kings, ruthless and determined in war, a strict observer of the Zoroastrian faith.

In the year A.D. 180 there was born to the high priest of the temple of Anahita in Istakhr, not far from the ruins of Persepolis, a son called Papak. We know little about the son, and still less about the father, who was called Sasan. We do know that Papak suddenly revolted against his overlord, the Prince of the province of Fars, and defied the Parthian Emperor to remove him from the provincial throne. The Parthian Emperor, busily fighting the Romans in the west, protested. He seems not to have been unduly perturbed. There had been rebellions before; they had been put down mercilessly. Papak's son, who bore the name of Artaxerxes, pronounced Ardashir in the local dialect, began rallying the people to his flag. With the blessing of the Zoroastrian priests, he overthrew the local barons and princes and marched north to Isfahan and Kerman. It was the beginning of the explosion which was to blast the Parthian dynasty from the throne.

Following the tradition of Cyrus, who rose out of a small community of dedicated men and in his own lifetime conquered most of the known world, Ardashir set out to conquer the Parthians and extend the borders of the Persian Empire. In three savage battles he defeated the Parthians, captured and killed the last Parthian King and would have killed all the Parthian Princes if

THE SPLENDOR OF PERSIA

some of them had not escaped to Armenia. He gave himself the title of "King of Kings of the Aryans," and not far from Persepolis, on a great bluff of yellow rock facing the Mervdasht Plain, at a place now called Naqsh-i-Rustam, he ordered a memorial of his triumph to be carved, so that his name and his victory should never be forgotten.

The carving remains, fresh and glowing in the sunlight, three times larger than life. A few yards away, hidden from the plain, are the tombs of the Achaemenian Kings, but Ardashir so placed this carving in his own honor that he acquires priority over the Achaemenians. He leads the procession. Almost casually, he has placed himself above all other Persian Kings.

In the carving, Ardashir shows himself receiving the diadem, the pledge of power, from the great god Ahuramazda. Both are on horseback. Under the horse of the King lies the last of the Parthian Kings, Artabanus. Under the horse of Ahuramazda lies "the one who lies," the devil Ahriman, with two snakes coming from his head. Behind Ardashir, holding a fly-whisk, is a guard, perhaps his son Shapur, which means "the son of the Shah." The god holds a sceptre, but no guard accompanies him, for he has no need of guards. There quietly, almost contemplatively, king confronts god. There is a strange tranquillity in the carving. Both king and god wear flowing gowns which hang in loose folds to the ground. Ribbons fall from the diadem, which is not incised deeply, but only suggested. The horses are not war-horses, but high-stepping ceremonial

THE SASANIANS

ponies. Once no doubt the carving was painted. We can guess the colors—the ring gold, the King's gown of purple ornamented with white, this being the color of the imperial robe of state of the Achaemenian Kings, the ponies white and spotless. Look at the carving more closely. The arms are elongated to suggest power, but it is power held in reserve. The bodies of the riders are supple—we shall see this same suppleness throughout the art of the Sasanian dynasty. In Achaemenian art the animals usually have more life than the men who stand beside them. Here the men completely dominate the animals. Part of the king's face has flaked away, but we can still recognize the face which meets us on the coins he issued: large eyes, a long, pointed nose, a curled beard woven in three long strands, an expression of extraordinary energy and concentration, as befits a man who believed himself touched by the divine radiance, without which no man can become a king.

Proud, imperious, determined to be at once King, Emperor, and High Priest of the newly created state, Ardashir concentrated all power in his own hands. Five and a half centuries had passed since the last of the Achaemenians perished, but he was determined to revive the glories of the past. "The King's power," he said once, "derives from his military power, and this can only be maintained by taxes, and all taxes in the end fall upon our farmers. It behooves us therefore to protect our farmers and treat them always with justice." These wise counsels he seems to have put into practice, for

THE SPLENDOR OF PERSIA

there is no evidence of rebellion within Persia during his reign.

Once he had conquered Persia, he gave himself the pleasant task of insulting the Romans and daring them to fight. To the new Roman Emperor, Alexander Severus, he sent a deputation consisting of four hundred of the handsomest young Persian noblemen riding their finest horses. This deputation demanded that all the captured property of the Persian King should be restored and that the Romans, who still possessed large outposts in Mesopotamia, should withdraw to Europe. It was a declaration of war, and Alexander Severus at once took to the field (A.D. 233).

If Ardashir hoped to drive the Romans out of Asia completely, he failed. Alexander Severus hated war, but he had steeled himself to fight, and accepted the challenge. There followed a series of confused wars on the borders of Persia, with neither side gaining any particular glory. Roman historians record that Ardashir went into battle accompanied by 12,000 horses in complete armor, 1,800 scythe-sided chariots and 700 elephants. These historians have been accused of exaggeration, but such a force is not improbable. After a reign of nearly fifty years, Alexander Severus held all the fortresses guarding the western approaches of Persia. The Romans still had their foothold in Asia. The Roman Emperor captured sufficient Persian booty to enable him to claim a victory, which he solemnly celebrated in Rome. The Roman army however was still based on Antioch-on-

THE SASANIANS

the-Orontes and the Romans governed only the fringes of Asia.

╂◦╂◦╂◦╂◦╂◦╂◦

WHEN Ardashir's son Shapur came to the throne, he had already been acting as regent for some years. He had a softer and fuller face than his father, but there was hard metal in him, and he had none of his father's intense feeling for Zoroastrianism. He first turned to the east. A long inscription at Naqsh-i-Rustam records his victories in northern India. He captured Peshawar, watered his horses in the Indus, crossed the Hindu Kush, conquered Bactria, and seized Samarcand. The Roman Empire was going through a period of convulsions. One after another, Emperors were being proclaimed, only to fall victim to paid assassins. Shapur marched west, conquered Armenia (which had long been the hereditary foe of Persia), invaded Syria, and captured Antioch, the wealthiest city of Asia and the chief Roman base. The Romans were compelled to fight or see all Asia Minor, Egypt, and perhaps Greece fall to the power of the Persians.

The Roman Emperor was Valerian, an old man, who had shown himself in the past a capable general. He was loved by his troops and feared by his enemies. But when he put himself at the head of a Roman army, he seems to have had a premonition of the fate in store for him. At the battle fought outside the city of Edessa, the ailing Emperor was captured alive, together with 70,000 Roman legionaries. The triumph of Shapur was com-

THE SPLENDOR OF PERSIA

plete. Never before had a Roman Emperor fallen into the hands of an oriental power. It is probable that the Emperor was put to death shortly after his capture, but for many years afterwards legend and rumor asserted that Shapur used the man as a mounting-block whenever he mounted his horse, the ailing Emperor bowing low to the ground and allowing his back to support the feet of the Persian King. They also say that when he died, he was skinned, and the skin was stuffed with straw. Then the stuffed Emperor was thrown into the corner of a Persian temple until he rotted away.

At Naqsh-i-Rustam, far in the south of Persia, and not far from the extraordinary monument which celebrates Ardashir's conquest of the throne, there is another carving in honey-colored rock celebrating the abasement of a Roman Emperor. Valerian kneels before Shapur, who rides a gaily caparisoned horse. The Emperor is very small, very tense, his arms thrust out as he pleads for mercy, his cape billowing, as though at that very moment, quite suddenly, at the prompting of the Persian King, he had fallen to his knees, and this very suddenness had sent the cape whirling. Shapur smiles down at him, one hand on his sword-hilt, the other raised in a gesture of triumph, his whole body assuming a pose of victory, while the great plumes above his crown climb so high that they thrust through the frame of the rock. Guards stand behind Shapur, impassive, impersonal. But these guards are only decoration. The artist has caught the moment of supreme victory and supreme abasement, and at first glance we

THE SASANIANS

are aware only of the two rulers confronting one another.

Shapur was so proud of his conquest of Rome that he caused four more rock carvings of the same scene to be made in the province of Fars. Some of these carvings are cluttered with the presence of the Imperial Guard, row upon row of them. It seems a pity. Such triumphs are more effective when depicted simply.

With this carving at Naqsh-i-Rustam there is the beginning of a purely Sasanian art. The old Achaemenian forms are preserved, but they are given more life. The sculptures of Achaemenian times have a strange stillness about them, as though life were welling up in the figures at noonday, quietly waiting to reveal itself: no one is in any hurry, all patiently await the word of the King. These Achaemenian faces are grave and mature: they have exhausted action, the world has been conquered, almost there is nothing left to do. But in Sasanian art the wind blows free, there is more light, more movement, more experiment. The swords flash in the sun. The Achaemenians seem never to have felt the need to depict a triumph with any sense of movement: it was enough to show the immense parade of soldiers and tribute-bearers. They had their settled faith in Ahuramazda. They had no restlessness. The Sasanians however were restless, delighting in movement, in the flow of draperies, in swift horses, sudden ambushes, quick alterations of mood. Their horses plunge headlong. They are on fire with the chase. Yet demonstrably

THE SPLENDOR OF PERSIA

they belong to the same race as the Achaemenians and worship at the same altars.

Restlessness drove Shapur again and again to the west. Having annihilated Valerian's army and driven his prisoners into Persia—they were made to build a city deep in the interior and place their knowledge and skills at the service of the Persians—he marched into Asia Minor, reversing the journey made by Alexander the Great. He passed through Cilicia, captured Tarsus and Caesarea, and was soon in the heart of Anatolia. Then he returned to Persia, his baggage-carts laden with treasure looted from the temples.

He was passing through northern Syria on his return to Persia when a curious incident occurred. Odainath, Prince of Palmyra, decided to send Shapur as a peace-offering a caravan of rich presents. Shapur, contemptuous of the powers of the small princeling, refused the gifts, asked insolently whether anyone had ever heard of Odainath and why he did not present himself in chains before the Great King. Odainath was infuriated. At the head of a small column culled from the villages and black tents of Syria, he proceeded to harass the immense army of the Persian King. His guerrillas fought the Persians as their Parthian overlords had fought the Romans. Shapur's soldiers were complaining. The army was weary of these pinpricks. Odainath's guerrillas seemed to arise from nowhere and vanish before anyone could tell from which direction their arrows had come. When Shapur reached the Euphrates and was crossing

THE SASANIANS

the river, the small column led by Odainath fell on his rear and captured part of the baggage-train laden with spoil from Asia Minor. Then, bearing their prizes, they vanished across the plain. Shapur was incensed, but there was nothing he could do, for his soldiers were in no mood for fighting guerrilla forces who possessed the gift of invisibility. He decided to bide his time.

In the end it was not the Persians, but the Romans, who destroyed the growing Empire of Palmyra. When Odainath died, his widow Zeynab (whom we know as Zenobia) saw her opportunity to drive a deep wedge between the Romans and the Persians. This cultured woman, who claimed descent from Cleopatra, led her armies into battle, and for a few brief years extended the power of Palmyra over the Middle East. She conquered Egypt, sacked Alexandria, and threatened both east and west, defying both the King of Kings—Shapur had given himself the title "King of Kings over the Aryans and over those who are not Aryans"—and the Roman Emperor as well. For a few months a Palmyrene Empire stretched from the Nile almost to the Hellespont. Soon a profoundly disapproving Roman Emperor appeared in Antioch, determined to put an end to this fledgling empire. He attacked her beautiful capital at Palmyra, where scholars from all over the world had been welcomed and where Longinus, who wrote *On the Sublime*, acted as her chief minister. Palmyra was well-defended. The Emperor Aurelian laid siege, but there were abundant supplies within the city. Suddenly and inexplicably the Queen's nerve failed and she slipped

THE SPLENDOR OF PERSIA

out of the city accompanied by a small guard, all on dromedaries. She was caught by some Roman cavalry and taken to Aurelian's tent. He treated her with honor, but led her in triumph through the streets of Rome when he returned to receive the honors bestowed on conquerors. She last appears in history as she shuffles in chains amid the crowds, half-fainting under the weight of her jewels, her golden shackles supported by a Negro slave. The Romans had pity on her and shouted that she must not be put to death, the usual fate of conquered rulers. After this brief appearance in the long procession which wound behind Aurelian's stag-drawn chariot, nothing more is heard of her except that she was allowed to live quietly in Tivoli and never returned to Palmyra.

The emergence of a Palmyrene Empire was a sign of the times: there was a kind of no-man's-land between the Persian and Roman empires which any small and determined state might conquer. There was no lack of candidates. The Armenians raided the territory; the Goths threatened it; obscure tribes of Arabs entered it. Then as now there were a host of small governments disputing among themselves for the privileges of conquest. Only Palmyra no longer threatened anyone: Aurelian sacked the city and razed most of it to the ground.

Of Shapur's last days we have only fleeting glimpses. Occasionally he can be seen adding to his grandiloquent titles, calling himself "Shapur, King of Kings, the god Ardashir, of the race of the gods, the offspring of the god Papak the King." He discarded Zoroastrianism. In

THE SASANIANS

its place he put Manichaeism, which had its roots in Zoroastrianism, but included a host of ideas from other faiths in a strange and powerful brew. Once Ardashir had said: "Consider the altar and the throne inseparable; they must ever support one another." And just as Ardashir was the high priest of the cult of Zoroastrianism, so Shapur proclaimed himself the protector of the Manichees.

Fifty years ago little was known about the Manichees; we owed most of our knowledge to the Christian commentators who recognized their seductive power and wrote impassioned pamphlets against a faith which threatened to sweep the world. The most illustrious of these commentators was St. Augustine, who once believed firmly in the tenets of this faith first announced by Mani on March 20, A.D. 242, the day of Shapur's coronation at Ctesiphon. On that day the twenty-six-year-old Mani began to announce the new religion to the crowds, declaring that he was the prophet.

꘎꘎꘎꘎꘎꘎꘎꘎

TODAY, from documents long buried in the sands, we have learned a good deal about the complexities of the religion which Mani preached and died for. He was born in Babylonia, of a prominent Parthian family, and trained as a painter. He had a high bulbous forehead, a straight nose, straggling mustaches and a little wisp of beard on his chin, and he is usually depicted in a mood of quiet contemplation, which is oddly at variance with his fiery writings. He called himself

THE SPLENDOR OF PERSIA

"the Ambassador of Light" and "the Paraclete," and believed that he alone had the power to separate the forces of darkness and light which ruled the world. He announced a new law: no living thing must be killed, there must be no falsehood, no fornication, no idolatry. As much as possible, men must free themselves from the temptations of the world. He called Jesus "the friend," but did not believe that Jesus suffered and died. His stern moral laws were made tolerable by the promise of a heavenly kingdom which would follow the final conflagration when darkness and light had shattered one another: then the Light would be redeemed, and irredeemable darkness would perish forever. All through his hymns there breathes the promise of the ultimate Light, the flare of God.

The strength of Manichaeism lay in its close-knit fabric, the sacraments of the bread and the wine, and its deep debt to traditional Persian influences. Somewhere in the mind of every Persian there was an awareness of the war between darkness and light: he was so accustomed to it that he could almost see the daily and nightly gathering of the forces of good and evil. But Zarathustra had never promised such a blinding victory for righteousness, nor had he endowed his priests with the gift of grace. The "elect" among the Manichees were themselves redeemers. The Manichees believed in prayer and fasting, and though they rejected image worship or any kind of statue, they left behind a number of illuminated manuscripts. Mani, a painter, is the only known founder of a religion who was a practicing artist.

THE SASANIANS

There was gentleness in Mani, and stubborn strength. He travelled widely, visiting western China and India. This new religion swept like wildfire. It became the state religion, to the despair of the Zoroastrians and Magians who fought him relentlessly and in the end succeeded in destroying him. When Shapur was dead and could no longer provide his protection, Mani continued to preach and send out missionaries, but he knew the time of martyrdom was drawing near. He was sixty when he was executed by Shapur's grandson, Bahram I. He suffered the fate of Valerian, his flayed body being stuffed with hay and set up over the gates of one of the royal cities. But with his death, his influence had only just begun. Not only St. Augustine fell under his influence. In India, in China, in the deserts of central Asia, and later in Syria, Bulgaria, Italy, and France his influence was felt. We can trace step by step how the Cathari and Albigenses in southern France derive from the teachings of a prophet who first announced his mission on the day of King Shapur's coronation.

With Mani dead, his followers driven out of the country, Zoroastrian became once more the state religion, upheld by the Persian Kings, who boasted how they had destroyed Manichaeism, Christianity, and Brahmanism within their empires. They needed to be stern, for they were being threatened on all sides; and Rome, as always, was threatening. The history of the Sasanian period is very largely the history of an endless war with Rome.

Again and again Persian armies set out for Antioch; again and again Roman armies set out for Ctesiphon,

THE SPLENDOR OF PERSIA

which had been the winter capital of Persia ever since
the Parthians first set up a vast camp facing the great
city of Seleucia, which itself seems to have been founded
on the site of Opis, where Alexander the Great first announced to a wondering world that Greeks and Persians
were brothers. For four hundred years, with rare intervals of peace, the war continued. Both Persia and Rome
were fighting for mastery of the Middle East, and neither
knew nor guessed that, in the end, an obscure tribe of
Turks from central Asia and a handful of Arabs striking
up from Medina far to the south would inherit the countries they had ravaged.

Roman historians have described the wars against Persia at great length, and they seem to have been perfectly
aware of the hopelessness of this conflict. Then, as now,
the world was divided between two great powers. Habit,
or instinct, or perhaps necessity drove them into permanent war.

The worst Roman Emperors continued the battle out
of a sense of duty. In A.D. 362 the young ascetic Emperor Julian the Apostate set out for Persia. He had
65,000 troops, and a fleet of 1,100 ships accompanied
him down the Euphrates. He was determined that this
should be the last invasion of Persia and he behaved
ruthlessly. He destroyed all the fortresses in his path.
The historian Ammianus Marcellinus reports how they
came to the city of Diacira. "We found it empty of inhabitants," he says, "but there was plenty of corn and
excellent salt. We burned the city. We found a few
women who had been left behind, and put them to

THE SASANIANS

death." Once again, as so often, the enemy was employing the "scorched earth policy": the Romans were continually meeting walls of flame from the crops set on fire by the Persians who were left behind. When he reached Ctesiphon, Julian found it curiously like the Roman palaces he knew, standing on a loop of the swift-flowing Tigris, shining in the sun, and apparently undefended. The King, Shapur II, was many miles away, trying to bring up his vast army in time. Julian saw the immense gardens reaching down to the river, and the zoo filled with wild animals for the King's amusement. He sent a detachment of cavalry to the zoo, and had the satisfaction of knowing that the King's collection of prize lions, tigers, and leopards had fallen to Roman swords. But it was more difficult to destroy Persian soldiers.

He waited a few days, retired, crossed the river, briefly fought a small Persian army which retired behind the walls of Ctesiphon—the Romans lost only seventy men in the engagement—and then after a brief attempt to besiege the city, he decided inexplicably to march eastward against the mountain provinces, first burning his fleet for fear it would fall into the hands of the enemy. It is possible that he was affected by the heat, but it is just as likely that he felt the wild exhilaration which comes with breathing the Persian air, and had not reckoned the cost. There followed an inevitable nemesis. He marched across the blazing desert to the Jebel Hamrin. His army was exasperated by the hovering mirages which appeared above the sand—all the mirages re-

THE SPLENDOR OF PERSIA

sembled Persian armies in formation, ready to attack. They suffered from thirst. They could not explain what they were doing there, and lost confidence in his leadership. In fact he was hoping to lead the Persian King into the defiles of the mountains, and trap him there. One morning he awakened and saw the whole Persian army waiting for him.

At daybreak, as far as the eye could see, the country glittered with their shining armor, and the cavalry in armor filled the plains and hills. And Shapur himself was there, mounted on his charger, and being taller than the rest, he led the army, wearing not a crown but a golden figure of a ram's head inlaid with jewels; being also splendid because of his retinue of noblemen and companions from all nations around him.

According to Ammianus, who tells the story, three pitched battles were fought. In the last battle Julian, who had discarded his cuirass because of the heat, was struck by a spear which embedded itself in his liver. He tried to draw the spear out, but it was sharpened on both edges to a razor sharpness, and his hands bled. He was carried dying to his tent, debating to the last with the philosophers he always brought in his train whether the soul was immortal. It was widely believed in Antioch that he was killed by one of his own men.

One after another, the Roman Emperors led their armies from Antioch and so to Carrhae and Ctesiphon, and then were thrown back. It was only when the two empires were coming to the end of their strength that

THE SASANIANS

they declared peace. In A.D. 545 Chosroes I, known as Nushirvan, meaning the Blessed, signed a treaty of peace with the Emperor Justinian. Then for fifty years there was no fighting between them. Many years after the long reign of Chosroes I came to an end, an obscure missionary in Arabia was asked for the date of his birth and answered: "I was born in the reign of the Blessed King." Mohammad, whose armies destroyed the Persian empire, was speaking of Chosroes.

✦✦✦✦✦✦✦✦

THERE WERE three supremely great Kings of Persia: Chosroes I was the second. He had a long, ascetic face and wore a look of extraordinary gravity at all times, but he was a man of peace. He surveyed the land, visited all the cities of the empire, saw that taxes fell equitably on the people. Vast numbers of Persians had died, and he placed the orphans in his personal care. He rebuilt the canals and restocked the farms, which had been destroyed in the wars. He built strong fortifications at the passes and placed subject tribes in carefully chosen towns on the frontiers, so that they could act as guardians of the state against invaders. Justinian paid him 440,000 pieces of gold, as a bribe to keep the peace, but he seems to have been a man who genuinely enjoyed the fruits of peace and saw no reason to continue a senseless war. He was tolerant of all religions, though he decreed that Zoroastrianism should be the official state religion, but he was not unduly disturbed when one of his sons became a Christian. He rebuilt the

THE SPLENDOR OF PERSIA

winter palace at Ctesiphon, and the great arch of his palace, called Takt-i-Kisra ("The Arch of Chosroes"), still remains and in its time was the widest single-span vault of unreinforced brickwork in the world.

In this vast palace Chosroes received the world's ambassadors and planned the defence of his empire, serving as King, high priest, and lawgiver. Stories were told of his nice sense of justice. Once an ambassador asked why the square in front of the palace was irregularly shaped. Chosroes answered that it could not be otherwise because part of this land was owned by an old woman who declined to sell at any price. He refused to force her to sell. Other stories were told of how he gave dowers to the poor, sent promising students to college, and sensibly discussed intricate problems of religion with foreign priests and philosophers. He set artists to work, for the country was now rich and huge wealth flowed into the imperial coffers.

The splendor of those last days of the Sasanian empire has become proverbial. Once again there was a flowering of taste. The quick curving dramatic line, which we associate with Sasanian art, seems to have reached its highest perfection during his reign. It was a time comparable to the Elizabethan period in England, the Renaissance in Italy, the reign of the Emperor Ming Huang in China. Tolerance, a delight in art, the coming of tradesmen and artisans from all corners of the world, innumerable translations of foreign works, Greek, Latin, and Indian, helped to foster an artistic rebirth. More than anyone else, by his character and his love of sump-

THE SASANIANS

tuous decoration and his instinctive understanding of
art, Chosroes seems to have been responsible for the
change. Yet to the end there was a curious remoteness
about him. He rejoiced in his majestic position and was
regarded by his subjects as though he were a god. He
sat on a golden throne, its legs inlaid with rubies. Above
his head, a gold crown hung from the immense vaulted
ceiling of the palace. Before him—the sign of his power
and wealth, and also of his priestly functions as one who
was in eternal communion with the god Ahuramazda
and could therefore bring seasonable weather to the
Persians—lay a great jewel-encrusted carpet representing a garden, the ground wrought in gold, the pathways
of silver, the blossoms, fruit, and birds in pearls, rubies,
diamonds, and emeralds. The carpet, which covered
nearly 1,000 square feet, represented spring, paradise,
majesty. A man seeing the King as he sat in cloth of
gold, blazing with jewels, with the carpet before him,
could not help being deeply impressed, seeing so much
glory and flashing fire at the King's feet. Costly draperies hung over the open archway. The walls were poly-
chrome stucco, painted over with immense murals.
Before the King, high officers of state, themselves on
fire with jewels, knelt in impassive splendor. Here for
the Persians and all the subject races lay the heart of the
mystery of Kingship, which the Sasanians, like the Achaemenians before them, elevated to the height of an
intricate and sumptuous art, to be imitated but never
rivalled by the Byzantine Emperors, who derived their
regal costumes and regal processions from the Persians.

THE SPLENDOR OF PERSIA

The habits and customs of royalty in the West derive straight from Persian models.

When Chosroes I died in A.D. 579, the influence of the Persians extended as far as Abyssinia and the Altai mountains on the borders of China; it reached down into India and included all Cappadocia and Syria. But already cracks were appearing. Once more the Romans were beginning to fear the expansion of Persia. There were border wars, the Turks were pressing down on the northern border, and both Persia and Rome found themselves looking apprehensively in the direction of the tribesmen pressing down from Central Asia. The Romans sent ambassadors to the mysterious figure who held the strings of power in the northwest. "In the valley of the Golden Mountain," they related afterwards, "we found the Great Khan in his tent, seated on a chair with wheels, to which a horse might be occasionally harnessed." In time, the Turks were to conquer Persia, but the real danger, unknown to anyone at Ctesiphon, came from the followers of the obscure missionary in Arabia. Within a few years of Mohammad's death the Sasanian Empire was to perish, while half of the Roman Empire was to fall into Arab hands.

Meanwhile Rome and Persia faced one another, supremely confident in the belief that they were the only two great powers and that one must destroy the other. The successor of Chosroes I was the young and talented Prince Hormizd, who found himself simultaneously at war with Romans, Turks, and Huns. Vahram Chobin, his greatest general, flung the Turks and Huns back into

THE SASANIANS

the arid wastes from which they sprang, but he failed to defeat the Roman legionaries. Hormizd, more scholar than strategist, ordered Vahram Chobin's abrupt dismissal. The general turned against the King, and the army made common cause with the nobles: Hormizd was dethroned in a palace revolution, thrown into prison, mutilated, and killed. His successor was Chosroes II, known as Parviz or "The Conqueror." With him the four-hundred-year-old dynasty went swiftly to its decline.

⊁⊙⊁⊙⊁⊙⊁⊙⊁⊙

IT WAS NOT the fault of Chosroes II, who had much of his father's studious intelligence and much of his grandfather's courage. He was determined to extend the borders of his empire. When the Byzantine Emperor Maurice was assassinated, he led his armies right up to Chalcedon, a suburb of Constantinople on the Asiatic side of the Bosphorus. He captured Antioch, Damascus, and Jerusalem, which he looted for three days. He carried a piece of the True Cross back with him to Persia. Shortly afterwards he captured Gaza and invaded Egypt. Once again the Persian Empire reached the extent it had reached under Xerxes. Flushed with success, he sent his armies again against Constantinople, but had to call off the siege. Then he retired to his new capital at Dastagerd which was adorned with silver columns and golden globes hanging from the ceiling. According to contemporary writers, his private game preserve included 960 elephants and 20,000 camels. Un-

THE SPLENDOR OF PERSIA

tramelled luxury invaded the court, and he is said to
have kept 12,000 women in his harem.

As he grew older, Chosroes II grew more grasping.
He had little of his grandfather's humility. A mass of
contradictions, he was graceful, generous, ill-tempered,
violent, murderous, and gentle by turns. He allowed his
beautiful Christian wife Shirin to build churches and
monasteries, but he massacred 50,000 Christians in Jerusalem and burnt the shrine of the Holy Sepulchre to the
ground. A famous story is told about his grandfather
Chosroes I, who once appointed an imperial paymaster-
general, saying that all the officials in the country must
be paid by the paymaster alone. Payments could be
made only on parade, and the officials must wear the
appropriate uniform. A few days later Chosroes I received an order from his own paymaster to appear on
the parade-ground. He rode up to the paymaster and
was properly inspected. It was discovered that he had
failed to bring with him the two extra bowstrings which
formed part of a mounted officer's equipment. Before
receiving his pay, he was sent back to the palace to find
the bowstrings, and it was only when he came back, his
equipment in order, that he received his pay. No one
would ever have told such a story about Chosroes II.

Legend has delighted to play with these two Kings,
affirming that benevolence was the mark of one, luxury
of the other. But legends often pardon the luxuries of
Kings. Innumerable poems and stories were written
about the devotion of the King to his wife Shirin, who
played polo and loved to hunt and sing and bestow her

THE SASANIANS

kindness on the people. Dark-haired, beautiful, with her mysterious smile and swaying walk, she peers at us from the countless miniatures made hundreds of years later by Moslem artists. Often these stories and paintings relate to the sculptor Farhad, who was so enamored of Shirin that he wandered disconsolately over the earth, carving her name in the rocks, till Chosroes II had pity on him and said if he would cut a water channel through a mountain of rock, he would surrender the Queen to the sculptor. When Farhad heard the false news of the Queen's death, he committed suicide on the mountain where he had hoped to carve the water-channel. "Farhad dropped tears of blood for Shirin's lips," wrote the poet Hafiz, and a hundred poets have imitated him.

It was a time of luxury, but also of delicacy, of simple vigor, of fierce hopes for the future. The gilded silver dishes with their portraits of Kings at the hunt are often overdecorated, but the lines are clearly drawn, and never lose their fluency. From the looms of Sasanian Persia came the patterned silks worn by Byzantine Emperors: Christian saints have been found wrapped in silken fabrics which show the characteristic patterns of Sasanian art—a King on horseback thrusting at lions, Princes on their thrones, medallions with animals shown always in pairs, facing one another and separated only by a flowering tree, which is the Tree of Eternity. These same motifs survived through the dynasties that followed.

Chosroes II had hurled down his gauntlet before Rome, and the Roman Emperor Heraclius hesitated be-

THE SPLENDOR OF PERSIA

fore picking it up. A sick man, suffering from dropsy, he was in no mood to begin a prolonged campaign. He began to build up his forces slowly. The loss of a piece of the True Cross had incensed Christendom; and when at last he struck against Persia, he was leading the first of the Crusades. But first he made common cause with the Turks, and in an incongruous scene the Great Khan prostrated himself before Caesar who then placed his own diadem on the Turk's head. The Great Khan promised to create a diversion in the eastern provinces.

With a huge army Heraclius descended on Persia. The Persian army was defeated amid the ruins of Nineveh, and then Heraclius advanced on Ctesiphon. Together with Shirin and three concubines, Chosroes fled, making his escape ingloriously through a hole in the wall, when he heard of Heraclius's successes. Dastagerd fell. The stars fought for Heraclius. The Tigris flooded, huge areas of Mesopotamia became marshland, and the army rose in revolt. Chosroes refused to surrender or sign a treaty of peace with Heraclius. A few weeks later he was killed by his son begotten by the Byzantine Princess Maria. The year after his death the Persian armies withdrew for the last time from Egypt and Queen Shirin placed in the hands of the Roman Emperor the piece of the True Cross which had been stolen so many years before.

Ten years before, Persia was the most powerful empire on earth. Now she was reduced to absolute anarchy. Kings and pretenders followed one another at a dizzy pace. In the space of six years the throne was occupied

THE SASANIANS

by five Kings, a general, and a daughter of Chosroes. In
the spring of 633 a grandson of Chosroes called Yezdegerd ascended the throne, and in that same year the first
Arab squadrons made their first raids into Persian territory.

It was the beginning of the end. Yezdegerd was a boy,
at the mercy of his advisers, incapable of uniting a vast
country which was crumbling into a number of small
feudal kingdoms. Rome no longer threatened. The
threat came from the small disciplined armies of Khalid
ibn Walid, once one of Mohammad's chosen com-
panion-in-arms and now, after the Prophet's death, the
leader of the Arab army. Ctesiphon was stormed. The
great carpet with its border of emeralds representing
green meadows and watercourses of pearls fell into the
enemy's hands and was cut up into small pieces, one
fifth going to the Caliph Omar, another fifth to Ali, the
son-in-law of the prophet, and the rest being divided
among the Arab soldiers. The great carpet was only part
of the plunder. There were vast stores of silver and gold,
costly robes, chests full of amber and musk, a horse
made of gold with teeth of emeralds, a ruby mane, and
trappings of gold. The armory of the Persian King contained a helmet, breastplate and greaves of solid gold
inlaid with pearls. All these were removed, until the
White Palace at Ctesiphon was stripped bare. Across
the sands innumerable camels carried the treasure away,
but the great palace, built of solid brickwork, hard as
iron, remained. Today only one crumbling wall and a
large part of the vaulted roof remain, and there is no

THE SPLENDOR OF PERSIA

longer any sign of the gold stars which were once painted on the blue vault and all the marble facing has disappeared, but like a huge and empty eye, the vault still looks across the plain, still terrifying in its splendor and its power.

After the Arab attack, Ctesiphon was never used as a palace again. The Arabs converted it into a mosque, and the banner of the Prophet hung where once had hung the banner of the Sasanian King.

For a little while longer the Persians fought back. But they were no match for the fanatical fury of the Mohamadans. In the battle of Nehavend in A.D. 642 the Arabs with an army of 30,000 destroyed a Persian army five times their number. Even then Yezdegerd fought on, never surrendering, refusing all offers of peace, rejecting all threats, maintaining the hopeless struggle for nearly ten years more, until at last he was assassinated near Merv. When Firdausi came to write the *Shah Nameh*, that immense epic describing the real and imaginary past of the Persians, he deliberately ended it with the death of Yezdegerd.

The empire fell. For eight hundred and fifty years the Persians were to be ruled by foreigners. In turn the Arabs, the Seljuk Turks and the Mongols ruled the land. The Sasanian empire survived in the hearts and the legends of the people. Ardashir, Shapur, Chosroes the Blessed, Chosroes the Conqueror, the beautiful Queen Shirin, and the tragic Yezdegerd lived on. In later years people came to believe that a daughter of Yezdegerd married Hussayn, the grandson of the Prophet Mo-

THE SASANIANS

hammad, and that somewhere in Persia, wandering mysterious and alone, there was an uncrowned King descended from this marriage who owed his title to his double descent from Mohammad and the Achaemenians. With every new conquering dynasty, the Persians fought back with peaceful weapons: they infiltrated the courts, and subtly influenced their conquerors, until the conquerors became more Persian than the Persians. Defeated for eight hundred and fifty years, they never recognized defeat.

THE SPLENDOR OF PERSIA

Persia under the Conquerors

A SMALL compact Arab army brought the Persian empire to its knees. Under a succession of great generals, the Arabs went on to conquer Egypt, North Africa, and Spain. Within a hundred years of the Prophet's death, they had forced their way into central France, the armies of the Moslems being defeated at last by

THE SPLENDOR OF PERSIA

the army of an obscure princeling, Charles the Hammer. The Persians fought with more slender weapons—scholarship, an unerring taste in art, a natural sense of supremacy. Soon the conquerors were conquered. A hundred years after the battle of Nehavend, Persian culture was making so deep an impression upon the Arabs that the marauding tribesmen were beginning to behave like Persians, wearing Persian clothes and reciting Persian poetry and subtly accepting Persian ideas. The world had been lost, only to be won again.

In nearly everything, the Persian temperament differed from the Arab temperament. The Persians were a settled people, who liked bright colors, flowing draperies, luxury after hard riding and hunting, the majesty of Kings. The Prophet said all men were brothers, the Prophet himself being brother to the meanest Negro slave, while the Persians wondered how a peasant could be the brother of a nobleman. They were feudal and caste-ridden and believed deeply in the portentous god-given powers of Kings, visible or invisible. They were both gay and disputatious by instinct, and did not take easily to dogma. For more than a thousand years they had worshipped fire and regarded the summer and winter palaces of their Kings as the centres from which the beneficent influence of Ahuramazda spread out like the rings on the surface of a pond when a stone is thrown into it. They were passionately fond of women, flowers, and animals. The stern morality of Mohammad met the fierce Persian delight in luxury, their love of the splendor in all created things. It was inevitable that Persian Mo-

THE SPLENDOR OF PERSIA

hamadanism would become, in time, profoundly different from the Mohamadanism practiced by the Arabs. In the end the Persians succeeded in inventing their own form of Mohamadanism, and in so doing they split the Mohamadan world in two. They set up their own places of pilgrimage and against the whole testimony of the Koran offered subdued worship to the descendants of the Prophet, and they continued to perform in the guise of a Mohamadan festival the great spring festival which was once performed by the Achaemenian Kings. To this day, the Arabs regard the Persians as heretics. The Orthodox Moslems call themselves *Sunnis*, meaning that they follow the *Sunna*, the remembered words and actions of the Prophet. Persian Moslems are called *Shia*, meaning "those who have broken away."

For about a hundred and fifty years after the Conquest, the Persians were governed by officers of the Mohamadan Caliphs, first from Medina and afterwards from Baghdad. These officers were determined to obliterate all vestiges of Zoroastrianism and of the Sasanian state. They destroyed and defaced, wherever they were able, the monuments of the Persian Kings. They milked the wealth of Persia. Arab armies were continually putting down small rebellions in Persia.

One circumstance helped immeasurably to unify the Persian spirit. Mohammad himself had never been on Persian soil, but his son-in-law Ali had fought in the wars of succession within the boundaries of the country. The Caliphate had passed into the hands of the Com-

PERSIA UNDER THE CONQUERORS

panions of the Prophet. Abu Bekr, Omar, and Othman had each briefly ruled over the empire of Islam. The Persians with their belief in the divinity of the sovereign adopted Islam, while refusing to accept the doctrine of the elective Caliphate. They believed that the Caliph, the spiritual and temporal ruler of Islam, must be descended from Mohammad or at least related to him by marriage. Accordingly, they regarded Ali, the Prophet's son-in-law, as their rightful King, and when Ali was stabbed to death in Kufa, their loyalty went to Ali's son, Hussayn. But the Ommayad Caliphs from their capital in Damascus were determined that the succession should remain in their hands. When Hussayn set out from Mecca to Kufa, expecting to be greeted with open arms by the people, an army sent out by the Ommayad Caliph was waiting for him. Hussayn was heavily outnumbered. On the night before the battle, Hussayn and his followers dug a trench behind them and filled it with burning faggots to cut off their own retreat. On the next morning, sword in one hand, Koran in the other, he led his followers against the enemy. One after another they fell to the Ommayad arrows, until only Hussayn remained alive. Two of his sons and six of his brothers lay dead around him when the Ommayads stepped forward to put an end to a life they had deliberately spared until the last moment. Then thirty-three Ommayad soldiers attacked him simultaneously, every man thrusting at him with a sword or a lance. They trampled on his body, cut off his head and brought it triumphantly to Kufa. There the governor of the city

THE SPLENDOR OF PERSIA

struck the head with his stick, and in the awful silence
that followed, an old man was heard saying: "Gently!
Alas, I have seen those very lips kissed by the Prophet
of God!"

A shudder ran through Islam. The Ommayad Caliph
soon came to realize the enormity of his crime. The
women who had accompanied Hussayn and his young-
est son were spared, and later sent back to Mecca, but
the harm had been done. On that day, the tenth day of
the month Moharran, Islam received its worst blow.
Henceforward "Revenge for Hussayn!" became the
watchword of the Shias, and every year in this same
month they performed the passion play describing the
death of the martyr Hussayn. Their most fervent wish
was to be buried near Kerbela, some sixty miles south
of Baghdad, where the tomb of the martyr was at once
a place of pilgrimage and an accusation against the
reigning Caliphs. For the Shiites, Kerbela remains the
holiest place in the world.

Hussayn was dead, but there still remained the descendants of his flesh. He was the first Imam, and all
his descendants in the line of succession were given this
title. The Shiites believe there have been twelve Imams,
and the last of them, Mohammad, is said to have disappeared somewhere within the city of Samarra about A.D.
874. They believe he is still alive and will return in the
last days, riding a white charger, to convert the whole
world to the Shiite faith. This twelfth Imam, also
known as the Mahdi, is the invisible and spiritual Emperor who rules over their lives.

PERSIA UNDER THE CONQUERORS

From Damascus, the Ommayad Caliphs, styling themselves the Vice-regents of God on earth and claiming spiritual powers as well as earthly dominion, continued to rule over the new Moslem empire which extended from Arabia to the gates of Constantinople. Cultivated and pleasure-loving, surrounding themselves with artists from Byzantium, Egypt, and Persia, strangely tolerant, they held power for nearly a hundred years. It was the Ommayad Caliph, employing Byzantine architects, who built the Dome of the Rock, wrongly called the Mosque of Omar, on the site where Abraham sacrificed the ram instead of Isaac and where Mohammad alighted on his mysterious night journey to Jerusalem and where once had stood the Temple of the Jews. Fourteen Caliphs followed one another on the throne of Damascus. Nearly all were able. Two, Abd-el-Malik and his son Hisham, would have been regarded as formidable and talented rulers at any time, ruling wisely, extending and strengthening the Moslem empire, cultivating the arts, building superb buildings which remain to this day as exquisite examples of architecture. Only the Persians, continually revolting in the distant provinces, seemed curiously lacking in respect for them.

Persia seethed with revolt. Conspiracies and secret societies abounded. A certain Abu Muslim, a Persian who spoke of himself as belonging to the Prophet's family, went about preaching the gospel of revolution against the detested Caliphate. At Merv he solemnly unfolded the black flag of the Prophet and announced the time had come to place on the Prophet's throne

THE SPLENDOR OF PERSIA

someone who was closer in blood than the reigning Caliph. He preached a revolution against the corruption of the Caliphate in the face of the misery of so many of the subject peoples. For his purpose he chose as the next Caliph a descendant of one of the Prophet's uncles, Abu'l-Abbas. The revolt succeeded. Under the genius of Abu Muslim, who went secretly about the country organizing the peasants and the landed gentry, a small secret society became overnight an army on the march. In 749, at Nehavend, where the Sasanian army was defeated a little more than a hundred years before, an Abbasid army surrounded and besieged the army of the Ommayads. The end of the Ommayads came soon after. The followers of the descendant of the uncle of Mohammad, led by Persian officers, began to hound and destroy the enemy like wild beasts. Not content with massacring the princes of the Ommayad dynasty, they opened up the graves of dead princes and Caliphs, nailed their long dead bodies to crucifixes and afterward burned them. All except two of the graves of the Caliphs were desecrated. The lone survivor, Prince Abd-ar-Rahman, a grandson of Hisham, succeeded in escaping to North Africa and later to Spain, where he inaugurated the new Ommayad dynasty which sprang up around Cordova.

꜠꜠꜠꜠꜠꜠꜠

THE NEW DYNASTY of the Abbasids was not Persian, but it came into power as the result of forces which had grown spontaneously out of the

PERSIA UNDER THE CONQUERORS

Persian character. Persians had led the revolt, financed it, and maneuvred the enemy into untenable positions. The ruthlessness of the Persians, avenging the death of Hussayn the martyr, led to the desecration of the Ommayad graves. Subdued for a hundred years, the Persians were beginning to exert their strength.

Gradually the new dynasty began to assume a purely Persian character. The new capital was Baghdad, not far from the imperial Sasanian city of Ctesiphon. Abu'l-Abbas, called "the Blood Shedder" from his success in exterminating the Ommayads, was followed by his brother Mansur, who elected to rule with all the trappings of a Sasanian King, wrapped in the inaccessible majesty of kingship. There had been times when the Ommayad Caliphs felt so secure they had wandered without guards through the streets of Damascus. All this was changed. The new Caliph could be approached only by specially privileged visitors who were compelled to crawl on their knees to the throne. A Caliph was on the throne, but, in fact, a Persian ruled. The Grand Vizier, Khalid, was the son of a Zoroastrian priest. Khalid and his son and grandsons became so powerful that no political action could take place without their consent. Incredible wealth poured into their hands, and it is from this family, known as the Barmecides because they were descended from a certain Barmak, that we derive the phrase "a Barmecide feast."

Under the Barmecides the position of Grand Vizier increased vastly in importance. They not only controlled the finances of the empire, but they commanded

THE SPLENDOR OF PERSIA

the army. They were the undisputed profferers of high honors and dignities. The Caliph himself withdrew from conduct of affairs, tending to live more and more in his harem. Whenever he appeared in public, he was followed by his chief executioner, and the leather mat for the victim's head always lay near the throne.

More and more, Persian habits and ideas invaded the court. Sasanian titles and forms of government were revived. Persian songs were sung, and Persian wines were drunk, and the courtiers wore Persian costume. Baghdad, built in the reign of Mansur, began to take on the aspect of a Persian city. It was given the name of Medina-es-Salaam, meaning the City of Peace, and for five hundred years under the Abassid Caliphs, the empire was at peace. There were countless revolts in Khorusan, sallies against Byzantium, raids against the Turks pressing down from the north, but on the whole, so great was the power of the Caliph and the Grand Vizier, that peace within the borders of the empire was maintained.

It was a time of luxury and extravagance and excitement, and at the same time, of a strange, wayward asceticism. The tall, dark, slender Mansur would shut himself up in his harem, enjoy all the delights which wealth and power could give him, and then suddenly spend days, weeks, and months in calm devotion to the Scriptures. He built magnificent mosques at exorbitant expense, but he took care through his Grand Vizier that the government was administered inexpensively, with the result that he earned the title of "Father of Farthings." Before he died, he ordered that a hundred tombs should be dug for him, so that no one would be able to desecrate his grave. None of these hundred tombs contained his body, for at his own wish he was secretly interred in another.

When his grandson, Harun al-Raschid, came to the throne, the family of the Barmecides was still all-powerful, though for a while they had suffered under two intervening Caliphs. Yahya, son of Khalid the Barmecide, was made Grand Vizier. He had been Harun al-Raschid's tutor, and the new Caliph always addressed him affectionately as "father." Yahya was one of the greatest administrators in history. He was tireless in building roads, he established order and security, and he had the Persian talent for spending splendidly but wisely. The empire prospered and literature flourished. Harun-al-Raschid had three boon companions: all were Persians. One was the scurrilous court poet Abu Niwas, the son of a Persian washerwoman. The others were Fadhl and Ja'afar, the sons of Yahya. Fadhl was appointed governor of the eastern provinces, a position of special trust. Ja'afar became the Caliph's confidant, the man with whom the Caliph delighted in wandering at night through the streets of Baghdad, both of them in disguise.

The Caliph's delight in the company of his favorite knew no bounds. Ja'afar was graceful, famous for his long neck and his dark gentle eyes. He was also an intelligent administrator, and could be ruthless in preventing the Caliph from exceeding the bounds of extravagance. Perhaps this was the cause of his downfall.

THE SPLENDOR OF PERSIA

Suddenly, without warning, Harun-al-Raschid (Aaron the Upright) had Ja'afar arrested. There was no trial. Ja'afar was beheaded. His head was placed on one of the bridges crossing the Tigris, and on two other bridges were placed pieces of his body. Yahya and Fadhl were flung into prison, and the Caliph confiscated the family fortune, which was said to have amounted to 36,676,000 dinars ($160,000,000). Some years later when a courtier was heard reviling the family of the Barmecides, Harun-al-Raschid said sharply: "Blame them less, or fill the gap they have left." In all the world no one ever received so costly and beautiful a robe of honor as Harun-al-Raschid once gave to his favorite. A surviving record from the Caliph's archives notes "400,000 pieces of gold for the robe of honor of Ja'afar, the son of Yahya the Grand Vizier."

The reign of Mamun, the son of Harun by a Persian slave-girl, began inauspiciously with wars on half the frontiers of the empire. There followed a long reign of peace, and now for the first time since the creation of the Abbasid Caliphate there arose a fierce intellectual ferment. The gates of European learning were opened wide. Aristotle, Ptolemy, and Euclid were translated into Persian and Arabic. Christians were allowed to discuss Christianity openly, and there were said to be 11,000 Christian Churches in the empire. It was the time of al-Kindi, the philosopher who first attempted to build a bridge between the learning of East and West, interpreting Aristotelian logic, adapting and modifying it, but always keeping in mind the need for cross-fertilization between Arabic tradition and Greek philosophy. He is half-forgotten now, but in his time he was a giant, and no one after him was ever so passionately concerned to marry Plato to the Koran.

The new inroads of western culture boded ill for the Persians, who saw their own influence at court receding. Worse still, in the reign of Mamun occurred the death of the saintly Imam Reza, the eighth descendant of Ali, and therefore to the Shias the most saintly person on earth, the true vice-regent of God. Imam Reza, married to the Caliph's daughter, was journeying with Mamun as the Caliph was making a tour of inspection of the eastern provinces. At a place called Sanabad the imperial procession halted, while plans were made for building a shrine in honor of Harun-al-Raschid. Imam Reza and Mamun—the young and saintly prince with the feverish eyes of the devoted servant of God, and the Caliph descended from the Prophet's uncle—were seen everywhere together. All Persian hopes were fixed upon the youth who wore only a loose white flowing gown and who seemed to possess the gift of performing miracles. It was said that he spoke in dreams with the Prophet, and that to touch the hem of his gown was to acquire eternal merit. He was more popular than the Caliph, for the very existence of the world hung on his lips. For the Persians the young Prince represented "the great King," the Father of all earthly creatures. He was the eighth of his line; there would never be more than twelve Imams, for had not Mohammad promised that the world would come to an end with the death of the twelfth, that there

THE SPLENDOR OF PERSIA

would be a blaze of fire, and Mohammad himself would once more appear among men, riding a white horse? Rumor, legend, or deliberate malice spread the story that the Caliph gave the Prince a bunch of poisoned grapes. All we know for certain is that he died suddenly and tragically, and in his honor the name of Sanabad was altered to Meshed, meaning "the place of martyrdom." Today this small city in northeastern Persia, close to the borders of Afghanistan, is accounted the most sacred spot on earth after Kerbela, where Hussayn met a martyr's death. The shrine at Meshed, lovingly and exquisitely designed, contains the bodies of Caliph Harun-al-Raschid and of the Imam Reza. Harun-al-Raschid lies somewhere under the pavement, but the tomb is unmarked—a sign of contempt.

By the fourteenth century, Meshed had become the most sumptuous, the most highly decorated, and the most revered of all Persian shrines. In 1601, the Emperor Shah Abbas did not think it beneath his dignity to walk the entire distance between Isfahan and Meshed in order to trim the thousands of candles in the sacred courts and acquire, at immense cost, the Koran said to have been inscribed in the Imam's own hand. The gravest claims were made for the pilgrimage to Meshed. It was recorded that Mohammad had once said: "A part of my body is to be buried in Khorusan, and whoever goes there on pilgrimage, Allah will surely destine to paradise, and his body will be *haram*, forbidden, to the flames of Hell: and whoever goes there with sorrow, Allah will take his sorrow away." Ali, the famous

PERSIA UNDER THE CONQUERORS

Commander of the Faithful, was even more explicit. He said of those who make the pilgrimage and earn the title of *meshedi*, "though their sins be as many as the stars, as the leaves of trees, they will all be forgiven."

Mamun ranks with Mansur and Harun-al-Raschid as one of the great Caliphs. He established observatories, encouraged music, allowed his court poet the utmost license to say what he pleased, and showed himself to be remarkably liberal. He seemed too to have a special affection for the Persians. He died at the age of forty-eight and was succeeded by his brother Mutassim, who lacked Mamun's *finesse*, his stern gaiety and his genius in inspiring affection.

Mutassim, the son of Harun-al-Raschid by a Turkish slave-girl, distrusted the Persians. He surrounded himself with a bodyguard of 4,000 Turkish soldiers who inspired such terror in the people of Baghdad that gangs went out to waylay them, knowing that they would probably be killed, but determined to put an end to "rule by 4,000 Turks." The Arab historian Yaqubi says that whenever it happened that one of the Turkish body-guard was killed, no one ever gave evidence against the perpetrators of the crime and everyone was secretly delighted. Frightened, clinging desperately to safety, Mutassim decided to place himself out of reach of his enemies. In A.D. 836 he removed himself from Baghdad and built for himself a new capital at Samarra, a few miles from the city. The Assyrian King Sargon had once done exactly the same thing, with disastrous effect. The new city, built on the site of a Christian monastery

THE SPLENDOR OF PERSIA

on the left bank of the Tigris, was occupied by eight Caliphs over a period of only fifty-six years, and was then abandoned. Today, the traveller in an airplane can see the outline of the city, the avenues and parks, houses, palaces, and mosques, very much as it must have looked from the air eleven hundred years ago, for everything is sharply and neatly delineated. But those who enter the fabulous city on foot see only ruins.

By leaving Baghdad, Mutassim placed himself at the mercy of his Turkish praetorian guard. Once again the Persians revolted. Delving deep down into memories of their past glories, sick at heart over the death of Imam Reza, they began to plan once more for the establishment of a purely Persian empire and chose as their leader a certain Babak, a follower of Abu Muslim, who wanted to abolish Islam and restore a mysterious "white religion." Babak raised the standard of revolt and there followed bitter fighting for three years, until Babak himself was finally captured, brought in chains to Samarra and solemnly executed. A revolt which was purely Persian in character had been put down with immense cruelty, but there were many more Persian revolts to come.

Until the end, Mutassim in his palace in Samarra remained a prisoner of his fears. Crafty and cruel, dependant upon his Turkish guards, incapable of governing, he was killed either by his own son or by one of the Turkish guards in his son's pay. Then, convulsively, the Abbasid empire began to break apart. There were continual border wars. The eastern province of Khoru-

PERSIA UNDER THE CONQUERORS

san fell into the hands of a local governor, who established his own reigning dynasty. Other provinces broke away. There were continual border wars. Descendants of the Sasanian Kings proclaimed themselves emperors, ruled briefly in the provinces and then vanished from the scene. There were annual raids by the Caliph's army into Asia Minor. The Turkish guards became arrogant. Mutassim's son, Mutawakkil, decided to act against them. Secretly, taking every kind of precaution, he prepared to slaughter them all. But at the last moment the secret was revealed to the guards, who murdered the Caliph. His son was murdered six months later. The Turkish soldiery had become the supreme power in the state, making and unmaking Caliphs at their pleasure.

All through these years the Persians continued to seek after power, maneuvering incessantly for position. In the reign of the Caliph Muqtadir (A.D. 908-932) the opportunity came. The Caliph, only thirteen years old when he came to the throne, fell under the influence of an aristocrat called Ahmad ibn Buwayh, who claimed Sasanian descent. Soon he was appointed "Amir-ul-Umara" or Commander-in-Chief. The Caliph became a puppet: all real power fell into the hands of the commander-in-chief. The family of the Buwayhids grew so rich and influential that it was able to send out its sons with the title of Sultans to rule all the chief cities of western Persia. All the land between the Caspian and the Persian Gulf fell under their control. They ruled wisely, endowed hospitals, created libraries. At

THE SPLENDOR OF PERSIA

any other time they might have succeeded in creating a purely Persian dynasty ruling over the whole empire, but already the country was crumbling. A bewildering number of rulers occupied the provinces, owing allegiance to the Caliph but otherwise possessing complete power over their own states. A puppet Caliph who insisted upon using his power would find himself abruptly removed, or blinded. At one period three former Caliphs were living in Baghdad, and all of them had been blinded to remove from them any of the temptations of power.

In such a situation the wretched remnant of the Abassid empire was in danger of being destroyed altogether by any foreign power which could send an army marching across Persia. In the reign of the Caliph Qa'im, the great grandson of Muqtadir, such an army appeared. The small native dynasties had already been swept aside by the emergence of the Persian Samanids, but these in turn had fallen to the Turkish princes who called themselves Ghaznevids. The new army, sweeping in from the northeast, made short work of the rivalries within the country, and soon the Seljuk Turks, from their pasturelands on the eastern shores of the Caspian, assumed complete control of the country.

✦✦✦✦✦✦✦✦✦

ONE DAY there appeared outside the walls of Baghdad the leader of the Seljuks with his army and his banners flying. The Caliph had been warned, and knew exactly what was expected of him as spiritual leader of the Abbasid world. He sat behind a screen,

PERSIA UNDER THE CONQUERORS

trembling, waiting for the moment when the conqueror would stride into the palace. The Caliph sat on a golden throne, wore the famous black mantle of the Abbasids and grasped the staff of Mohammad in his right hand. The Turkish chieftain knelt, kissed the stones at the foot of the Caliph's throne, went to a throne especially erected for him and listened carefully while one of his lieutenants announced that he, the tribal chieftain from Turkestan, had come to inherit the temporal rule of the empire. Thereupon he was invested with seven robes of honor, and presented with seven slaves, representing the seven provinces of the empire. He wore a veil to hide the splendor of his face from the mere courtiers, and this was solemnly sprinkled with musk; then two crowns were placed on his head, and he was given two swords to symbolize that he had become King of East and West, a title now bequeathed to him by the Caliph. Receiving the swords, the young chieftain attempted to prostrate himself before the Caliph, whose spiritual power he acknowledged; but servants and ministers hurried forward to prevent him. Then he kissed the Caliph's hand, and his name and titles were shouted to the people by heralds.

The name of the young Seljuk Prince was Toghrul Beg. Of all the invaders of Persia, he and his descendants alone are regarded tolerantly by the Persians.

Toghrul Beg died shortly after coming to power, being succeeded by the brilliant and handsome Alp Arslan, a tall man famous for his skill at archery and for his mustaches which were so long that they had to be tied

THE SPLENDOR OF PERSIA

up whenever he went hunting—until quite recent times these immense mustaches, stretching sometimes to the length of two feet, have been the hallmark of Persian Kings. He enjoyed the distinction of capturing a Roman Emperor, Diogenes Romanus IV, who fell into his hands at the battle of Manzikert. According to Persian historians, Romanus had taunted the Seljuk King, saying: "If this barbarian really desires peace, let him come over to my camp and solemnly surrender his palace at Rayy as a pledge of sincerity." Thereupon Alp Arslan is said to have fallen to his knees in prayer and afterwards put on a white gown, perfumed himself with musk, surrendered sword and spear for mace and scimitar, and promised he would not leave the field alive unless he won a victory. There was a hard-fought battle, and by nightfall the Emperor Romanus, his horse dead, himself wounded, his army destroyed, waited for whatever might befall him. He was seen by a slave who had remembered how he looked on the throne at Constantinople and by a strangely deformed soldier. The successor of Constantine was led by these two captors to the tent of Alp Arslan and forced to kiss the ground at the foot of the throne. A moment later Alp Arslan leaned forward and raised the Emperor up, thrice clasping his hand and promising that his life and dignity would be spared.

"I would like to know what you would do, if you were in my place," Alp Arslan asked.

"I would beat you to death with whips," Romanus answered.

PERSIA UNDER THE CONQUERORS

The honest answer pleased Alp Arslan, who had the satisfaction of being able to remind the Christian Emperor about Christian principles, saying over and over again how much it pleased him to be merciful. At the cost of an enormous bribe, the surrender of all Moslems then in the hands of the Greeks, and an annual tribute of 360,000 pieces of gold, Romanus was allowed to go free.

Alp Arslan was not always so generous. He was leading a punitive expedition against some tribes in Transoxiana when he met his death. He had crossed the Oxus and was installed in his camp when the captain of a newly captured fort forced his way into the Sultan's tent. The man was insolent, tempers flared, and suddenly Alp Arslan ordered the man to be impaled. The unfortunate captain broke out into loud curses. Alp Arslan grasped his bow and shot at him, but the arrow went wide. Suddenly the captain sprang on the Sultan, slashed at him with a dagger and fatally wounded him. Four days later Alp Arslan died. The captain had been cut to pieces by the Sultan's guards.

It was a time of splendor, of wide-ranging conquests, of a curious marriage between Persia and Turkestan. Alp Arslan succeeded in regaining Mecca and Medina for the empire. He recovered Aleppo. Above all, he cherished artists and poets, and the pottery and architecture of his time have a wonderful glowing spontaneity. When he died, he left behind the epitaph which he himself chose for his tomb. It read: "O ye who have

THE SPLENDOR OF PERSIA

seen the glory of Alp Arslan exalted to the skies, repair to Merv and behold it buried in the dust."

Alp Arslan was succeeded by his son Malik Shah, who extended the boundaries of the empire as far as the mountains of Georgia and the walls of Constantinople, Jerusalem, and all Arabia. Austere and tolerant, brilliantly assisted by a famous Grand Vizier called Nizam-ul-Mulk, Malik Shah ruled benevolently. He patronized Omar Khayyam and built hospitals for the poor. He entrusted high offices to Persians. To safeguard the dynasty he married the daughter of the Caliph, and for a while thought seriously of abolishing the Caliphate, which had long outlived its usefulness. In his reign the Seljuks entered into their golden age, and in this same reign the two forces which were to destroy the Seljuks began to prepare their engines of destruction—the Assassins and the murderous Mongol horde were already at work.

✦❖❖❖❖❖❖❖❖❖

THE Assassins derive their name from the hashish which they smoked or drank to make them reckless in war. They formed a heretical sect, denying both the Sunni and the Shia beliefs and holding that the succession of the descendants of Ali, the Prophet's cousin and son-in-law, ended with the seventh Imam whose name was Ismail. Several mountain strongholds fell into their hands, the most important being Alamut, meaning "the Eagle's Nest," north of Kazvin. There

PERSIA UNDER THE CONQUERORS

under a leader who came to be called "the Old Man of the Mountains" fanatical believers in the Ismaili faith were trained in the use of arms and in the arts of disguise. These mountain strongholds, high up and hidden from the roads, were soon filled with young men converted to the faith, more fanatical than their teachers because they were converts. They were taught foreign languages, so that they could go about their errands in foreign countries; they swore oaths of undying loyalty to their leaders. They were trained assassins, with a very brief expectation of life. Legends grew up around them, and it was said they were drugged with hashish, then taken to beautiful gardens filled with flowers and dancing-girls and told that they were in heaven. This paradise had been granted to them by the power of "the Old Man of the Mountain"; and if they wished to enter this paradise for the rest of their lives, then they must accomplish the difficult tasks commanded of them. Then stealthily they climbed down the mountain and committed their murders. The most important of their victims were two Caliphs. The most defenceless was the aged Nizam-ul-Mulk, who at the age of ninety-three, having recently retired from the service of the Sultan, fell to an Assassin's dagger.

The terror of the Assassins was felt throughout the empire; it reached into Syria, where they formed small bands of determined warriors fighting against the Crusaders and had their own mountain strongholds. Their will was law, and the Seljuk Kings fought against them in vain. By an odd chance, the wealthiest and best pro-

THE SPLENDOR OF PERSIA

tected of the Assassins' strongholds was in the path of
the Mongol chieftain Hulagu when he swept down on
Persia. Alamut was destroyed. The Mongols, more
murderous than the Assassins, marched on to Baghdad.

None of the assassinations of the Assassins were of
much consequence compared with the massacres of
Hulagu. The Mongols were the most completely merciless people the world has ever seen. Baghdad was besieged, and on February 10, 1258 was compelled to surrender. Caliph Muttasim walked slowly out of the gate
into the enemy lines, accompanied by his three sons.
There followed a week of slaughter and there is no reason to disbelieve the claim of the Mongol historians that
800,000 Baghdadis were killed. The corpses of 700
women and eunuchs were dragged out of the Caliph's
harem before Hulagu put up his tent there. A vast treasure of gold and silver rose like a mountain around his
tent. Then when the treasure was removed, the city was
put to the flames. The Caliph and nearly all his family
were slain.

Under Hulagu, the Persian empire extended from
the Mongol dominions in the north to the borders of
Egypt. Tribute was paid to the Great Khan. Islam was
frowned upon, and Baghdad itself became no more than
a provincial town after rising from its own ruins. Mara-
gha in northern Persia became the new capital of the
empire. Against the strange shamanism of the Mongol
conquerors, the Persians possessed no weapons. For
seventy weary years they suffered under a succession of
Mongol princes. One, known as Sultan Uljaitu, was con-

PERSIA UNDER THE CONQUERORS

verted to the Shia creed and even stamped his coins with
the names of the twelve Shia Imams. Slowly the Persians were gathering their forces, plotting to conquer
their conquerors.

The disasters of Hulagu's conquest were followed
by the worse disasters of Timuri Lang or Tamerlane,
greatest and cruelest of the Mongols, whose long reign
—he died at the age of seventy—was marked by continual massacres. Where the first Mongol wave had
never penetrated, Timuri came with his soldiers and executioners like someone intoxicated with destruction.
All that had been patiently built anew after the invasion
of Hulagu was now destroyed. This time the invader
paid special attention to south Persia. Isfahan was destroyed: at its gates, Timuri feasted on a spectacle of
70,000 skulls formed into a pyramid. Only once did
he nearly lose a battle. This was outside Shiraz where
Mansur, Prince of Fars, joined battle with him. A sudden Persian onslaught drove through the ranks of the
Mongols. All except fifteen of Timuri's guards were
cut down, and the Mongol prince received two deadly
blows on his helmet from a scimitar. Persian historians
like to say that at this point Timuri escaped into the
women's quarters and hid behind the skirts of his concubines. A few hours later the tide of battle had turned.
The Mongols broke the Persian ranks and destroyed
their army. Timuri casually ordered that every single
male child and every Persian man must be put to death.
Once again Baghdad was sacked. Thousands were massacred, immense wealth was taken away, all the mosques

THE SPLENDOR OF PERSIA

and schools were destroyed, but the splendid heaps of gold vessels which had been piled up for Hulagu were absent: Baghdad had never recovered from its wounds. Then Timuri went on feverishly to extend the bounds of his empire.

With the successors of Timuri weariness set in: the thirst for conquest had been sated. If there were no peace in the country, at least there was a period of relaxation in which the architects could design an astonishing series of magnificent buildings, mosques, and schools raised to the glory of the Timurids. At Samarcand, at Herat, in a hundred other places they built nobly, cultivated the poets and practiced the arts of peace. By a convenient fiction the great blood-letting of the time of Timuri was forgotten by his descendants, Shah Rukh and Sultan Hussayn. It was the time of the poet Jami and of the painter Bihzad. The storm was over, and an uneasy peace took the place of war.

The Timurid dynasty, which had begun so fearfully, followed a familiar pattern. The Persians won over their conquerors. Sultan Hussayn, the last of the Timurid princes, composed a curiously ornate work entitled *Ponderings upon Mystic Lovers*. It is unlikely that the tall, gangling, limping murderer we know as Tamerlane would have approved of the writings of his descendant.

Wave upon wave of invaders had descended upon Persia, coming from the shores of the Caspian or out of central Asia or from Arabia, and all in time had fallen under the spell of the Persians, learned the Persian lan-

PERSIA UNDER THE CONQUERORS

guage, adopted Persian manners, cultivated Persian arts. Innumerable wars were fought, towns fell, all their inhabitants were massacred, and yet Persia continued to exist, uplifted by an immense spiritual vitality. Compelled to accept foreign doctrines, the Persians improvised, played for time, conveniently translated and transmuted the alien element until it took on the appearance of something they had themselves invented, so that even Islam failed to conquer them and they adapted it for their own purposes, making it more mysterious and poetical, and altogether more Persian. There is Tamerlane gazing calmly on the mountain of skulls, and just as calmly Sultan Hussayn composes poetry in a court given over to poets, as the Timurid dynasty falls slowly to its decline. The genius of the Persians was in their power to absorb all foreign influences and subtly transform them. At their worst times, when the country was split apart at the mercy of marauding armies, they produced their greatest poets.

THE SPLENDOR OF PERSIA

The Persian Poets

ALL THROUGH the literature of Persia there has been a current of mysticism. The gay, enquiring minds of the Persians were rarely satisfied with the stern dogmas of Islam and they rebelled against the austerity of Zara-thustra. They delighted in physical things, while at the same time thirsting for God, and it was inevitable that they should find their keenest pleasure in combining their awareness of God with a daily delight in the world around them. So there grew up in Persia the extraordinary movement known as Sufism from the simple woolen robe (*suf*) worn by the wandering monks who were the first to celebrate a profound reversal of the dogmas of Islam. And to understand Persian poetry we must glance briefly at that movement which was so closely identified with it.

We know very little about the origins of Sufism except that at some time in the eighth century, about a hundred years after the Moslem conquest of Persia, a small sect broke away from orthodox Mohamadanism and announced its opposition to all the rituals and ostentatious ceremonies in the mosques. For the first time there began to be heard the words: "Obey no dogmas! Attend no ceremonies! Mohammad said that Allah is as close to a man as his own neck vein, but we say that he is even closer—he is deep in our hearts!" The Sufis proclaimed that God was in everything, and far from being unapproachable, as the Koran declared, He could even be seen by mortal eyes. There were some Sufis who declared that the world was made by God for the delectation of man and should be enjoyed to the uttermost. There were others who loved the world so little that they spent their days praying for Paradise. Perhaps the mood of the Sufis can best be demonstrated by the celebrated prayer of one of the earliest, the saintly woman, Rabi'a al-Adawiyya (717-801) who wrote:

THE SPLENDOR OF PERSIA

O God, if I worship Thee in fear of Hell, burn me
in Hell; and if I worship Thee in hope of Paradise, ex-
clude me from Paradise; but if I worship Thee for Thine
own sake, withhold not Thine Everlasting Beauty.

It was the same astonishing woman who wrote towards the end of her life:

Dear God, give to Thine enemies whatever Thou
hast assigned to me of this world's goods, and to Thy
friends whatever Thou hast assigned to me in the world
to come; for Thou Thyself art sufficient for me.

The prayers of the Sufis were often as simple and
demanding. The Sufis are overwhelmed by the near
presence of God and desire nothing more than to share
their knowledge of God with others. God was close
to them, so close indeed that they regarded religious
ceremonies as getting in the way; and because they
celebrated the presence of God in all things, they saw
no reason for celebrating Him particularly at various
ordained hours of the day. They laughed at Moslem
scholars just as they laughed at pilgrimages to Mecca.
Was not every journey—even a journey across a room
—a pilgrimage to some object which had been hallowed
by God? They took very seriously the text from the
Koran: "Wheresoever you turn, there is the face of
God."

Such beliefs, by their very simplicity, struck at the
heart of orthodox Mohamadanism. The Sufis opposed
all rituals, all theological complexities. Like Søren

THE PERSIAN POETS

Kierkegaard, the Danish theologian of the last century, they proclaimed that the Knight of the Faith might be the little tobacconist who keeps the corner shop and takes his wife out for a stroll in the park every Sunday afternoon. It was not by intellectual attainments nor by profound obedience to the Church that men came to God: they came to God because they quietly and unobtrusively dedicated themselves to God. Indeed, there was one school of Sufis which declared that every act of religious ostentation was suspect, and the truly devout man would disguise himself as a thief or a brigand in order to be sure that no act of his would be regarded as that of a devout man. "Conceal your virtuous actions at all costs," said one famous Sufi who was known as "the barefoot monk." "If it should happen to you that men think you are a thief, then deliberately wear the disguise of a thief." He declared that there was more consciousness of God among vagabonds, cut-throats and murderers than among the people who were usually regarded as devoted followers of Mohammad.

The Sufis regarded the Koran with reverence, but allowed themselves to interpret the texts allegorically or in any way they pleased. They laughed away some of the stern injunctions of Mohammad. Though they called themselves "men of the wool," they thought of themselves as swordsmen who had cut through the intricate knots of theology. According to them, it was nonsensical to devote one's life to the solemn elucidation of Koranic texts. Quite suddenly, if one opened one's eyes very wide, a man would see the world as it truly

THE SPLENDOR OF PERSIA

is, shining in the light of God. Beyond this it was unnecessary to go, for the fullness and perfection of God could be known even to a little child.

There was very little in Sufism which was completely original. Similar movements had arisen many times in the past as a reaction against rigid orthodoxy. What was new was the peculiar Persian coloring they gave to their faith. Under Islam the Persians found themselves strait-jacketed, their mercurial minds at odds with strict dogma and absolute protestations of faith. Characteristically they had refused to accept the elected Caliphs, they had kept faith with the descendants of Ali and they had come to regard a mysterious "Hidden Imam" as the successor of Mohammad. Sufism is colored by the Persians' tolerance and by the glitter of their skies. Of the great Persian poets following the Conquest, all except one were Sufis.

Because the Sufis demanded the utmost freedom in their forms of worship and deliberately opposed the mullahs, they were often brought before the religious courts, ordered to confess, and tortured to death. There was a long line of Sufi martyrs. Martyrdom however only increased their numbers. They were fearless in their championing of the Sufi faith. In time so many Persians became Sufis that the religious courts no longer prosecuted them. Their lack of orthodoxy became another orthodoxy; and in the religious history of Persia some of the Mohamadan saints were Sufis.

Though the Sufis were forever displaying their horror of the discipline of the established Church, it would

THE PERSIAN POETS

be a mistake to assume they were lacking in discipline.
They invented their own harsh regimens. Though
many lived in the world, others succumbed to a monk-
ish habit of living quietly in cells, eating little—a
few chickpeas a day, and a cup of water—and continually praising God and celebrating His glory. At some
period in their lives nearly all the Sufis fasted and
mortified their flesh. Many married and lived outwardly
normal lives, while others took the vow of celibacy.
The saintly Rabi'a al-Adawiyya refused all offers of
marriage, saying that since she existed in God, the
marriage contract must be asked of God, not of her. All
Sufis purified themselves by a long and arduous training
in meditation and prayer. A novice was taught to
abandon all his personal desires, even the desire for
salvation and the mystical union with God. The perfect Sufi must love God for His own sake, without
hope of reward. He must ask for nothing, since God,
the Giver, is greater than all His gifts.

✦✦✦✦✦✦✦✦✦

STRANGE TALES were told about the early
Sufis. There was the saintly Bayazid (Abu Yazid), the
first of the "God-intoxicated" Sufis, who was transported on the wings of mystical fervor and suddenly
announced to his disciples: "Behold, I myself am become God! There is no other God but Me! Glory to
Me! How great is My Majesty!" Usually the disciples
refused to be embarrassed by these ecstatic utterances,
interpreting them as innocent of blasphemy. So a man

THE SPLENDOR OF PERSIA

might speak when he comes face to face with God. But he had never spoken the words with such authority before, and when he came out of his mystical trance they told him exactly what he had said. Bayazid was shocked. He said: "If you ever hear me speaking like this again, then kill me!" The disciples sharpened their swords. They had been taught instant obedience to the master. A few days later Bayazid fell into another ecstatic trance and was heard saying: "Whether you seek God on earth or in Heaven, you will only find Him beneath my garments!" The disciples struck, thrusting their swords into his body. Instead of killing Bayazid, the swords curled back and wounded the disciples. When Bayazid recovered from his trance and learned what had happened, he explained that his body had become in a state of trance like a pure mirror, and those who struck him saw their own faces in the mirror and so wounded themselves. "My soul," he said, "had departed from the mirror of my body and was one with the Beloved." Such at any rate is the story which was believed by the Sufis, who worshipped Bayazid this side of idolatry.

The stories about Bayazid are legion, and it would be easy to disbelieve them if his own writings did not confirm them. He is among the best, and most authoritative, of Sufi theologians. He declared that he had seen God many times, and reading his own account of his ascent towards God's shining face, it is hardly possible to discredit him. He speaks quietly and calmly about things one would have thought it impossible to write about. It was to him that the Sufis owed the doctrine of the annihilation of the self (*fana*), which from his time onward assumed a central position in Sufi thought. To Bayazid, too, belong the famous words: "I am become the wine-drinker and the wine and the cup-bearer."

✦✧✦✧✦✧✦✧✦

ABOUT the year A.D. 874, when Bayazid died, there was born in Baghdad to the son of a woolcarder a boy who was given the name Mansur al-Hallaj. He was small, dark, and seemed to have no strength in his body. He was reputed to possess magic powers. He visited India, where he reported that he once saw the famous Rope Trick performed by a woman. One day after his journey to India, he stretched forth an empty hand in the air and produced an apple from an invisible tree, saying he had plucked it from the tree of paradise. One of the disciples pointed out that the apple was full of maggot-holes and al-Hallaj laughed, saying, "How could it be otherwise? I plucked the tree from the Mansion of Eternity and brought it into the House of Decay, and that is why it is touched with corruption!"

He was almost the first Sufi to argue against making pilgrimages to Mecca. Orthodox Islam was prepared to give the Sufis unusual tolerance, but not when they preached fundamental heretical doctrines. He was arrested, imprisoned, and tortured. He was ordered to disavow his heresies. He had proclaimed that a saint, in his mystical union with God, was infinitely superior

THE SPLENDOR OF PERSIA

to a prophet, by which he meant the Prophet Mohammad. Against the whole weight of the Koran he declared
that man was created in the image of God so that he
could love God in the divinity within himself. A hundred other heretical opinions were credited to him. It
was decided to crucify him. When he was brought to
be crucified and saw the cross and the nails, he showed
no fear. He was heard uttering the prayer which became
famous among the Sufis:

> O Lord, have mercy on the people who desire to
> slay me; for truly if Thou hadst revealed to them what
> Thou hast revealed to me, they would not have done
> what they have done; and if Thou hadst hidden from me
> what Thou hast hidden from them, I would not be suf-
> fering this tribulation. Glory unto Thee whatsoever
> Thou doest, and glory unto Thee whatsoever Thou will-
> est!

For four days, al-Hallaj hung on the cross beside the
Tigris. When at last he was taken down, close to dying,
he was heard to say that he had felt neither pleasure
nor pain, only the overwhelming love of God.

Ten years later, because he continued with his heretical beliefs, it was decided to put an end to his life. He
was completely reckless and refused to ask for mercy.
For his heresies he was scourged with a thousand stripes,
and for refusing to abjure them, he was sentenced to be
burned to death. Just before he died, he told his disciples that he would return in thirty years, exultantly
reciting his own poems.

THE PERSIAN POETS

ABU SAID IBN ABI 'L-KHAYR (967-1049)
was born in Khorusan to a family of weavers. When he
was quite young, he became the pupil of a famous Sufi
master. He was infinitely obedient to his master until
one day it suddenly occurred to him that it was absurd
to be following in the footsteps of a saint and it would
be better if he lived the life of a Sufi among ordinary
people. "The true saint," he said, "goes among the people, and eats and sleeps with them, and buys and sells in
the market-place and marries and takes part in social
life, and never for a single moment forgets God." He
lived quietly in Khorusan, spending his days going about
ordinary affairs and poring over the Koran. One day
when he was twenty-six he was attending the lectures
of the famous mullah, Abu Ali, who was discoursing
on the text from the ninth verse of the sixth book of the
Koran: "Lord, may they amuse themselves with their
vain discourses." It occurred to him that the mullah
himself was merely amusing himself with vain discourses. This thought came to him in a flash of lightning. From that moment he threw his books away. "The
first step," he wrote, "is to burn the books, destroy the
inkpots, and forget everything you have learned." He
retired to a small corner of his own house, which he
converted into a chapel. There he remained for seven
years, continually repeating the Holy Name, thus following in the path of Bayazid, who believed that the
ceaseless repetition of the Holy Name would bring

THE SPLENDOR OF PERSIA

men into direct communion with God. He became an ascetic. He mortified his body. He wore the same shirt until it fell to pieces. He ate nothing until sunset, and then only a piece of bread. He never lay down to sleep, but fashioned a small niche in the room which would support him standing through the night. He stopped up his ears so that no sounds would disturb him. One night he hung himself upside down in a well and recited the whole of the Koran before he came up again. He was always begging to be allowed to perform small services for other Sufis, and would sometimes ask them to let him clean out their privies.

Abu Said was the completely "God-intoxicated" man. It would come to him sometimes to sing hymns all day and all night, and he would be singing hymns when his voice was no more than a feeble hoarse whisper. Suddenly, at the age of forty, he abandoned his quest for direct communion with God and became the abbot of a monastery, busying himself with practical affairs. He became a hard task-master and wrote for the monks a stern code of laws in which all their actions were minutely regulated. The wheel had turned full circle. The man who had once wanted to burn the books and forget everything he had ever learned was busy writing books and seeing that the monks learned from them.

As we watch the Sufis wandering down the dusty roads of Persia, they seem not to belong to the earth. There is a brilliant light in their eyes, and sometimes their mouths twitch. It was as though in them the or-derly processes of thought had been exchanged for ec-

THE PERSIAN POETS

static visions. They were more like poets than theologians, more like heroic adventurers than practical men of affairs. They were men of large character and a strange wayward grace, devoted to God and in love with the electric world they saw with their eyes—a world which seemed to them to be peopled by angels who lived happily in cities built of crystal. Reading them, we are aware of their intense joy and of the joy they gave to others. In feeling and in utterance they were close to the English poets Henry Vaughan and William Blake:

> *I saw eternity the other night*
> *Like a great ring of pure and endless light . . .*

> *To see a world in a grain of sand,*
> *And a heaven in a wild flower;*
> *Hold infinity in the palm of your hand,*
> *And eternity in an hour.*

For them, as for Vaughan and Blake, eternity was always just around the corner and at any moment, looking at a flower or a beloved face or a sunset, they would see the face of God. Like Shelley they regarded the mind of man as "a mirror of the fire for which all thirst."

The Sufi beliefs grew out of the tragedy of the times, but in a sense they had always been present in the Persian spirit. The delicacy, the rapture of adoration, the sense of identity with the visible world, itself no more than an emblem of God's majesty, all these things were already present. It follows that the most Persian of poets

THE SPLENDOR OF PERSIA

should be the most mystical, the one most saturated
with the knowledge of God.

╾◌╾◌╾◌╾◌╾◌

JALALU'L-DIN RUMI was born at Balkh
in the northern province of Khorusan in A.D. 1207. At
that time the province was under the rule of a certain
Shah Mohammad, who ruled an empire extending from
the Ural Mountains to the Persian Gulf, and from the
Indus almost to the Euphrates. The Caliphate was in
decline: half a dozen princes ruled over its several parts,
all fighting for mastery, unaware that they were about
to be swept aside by the Mongols beyond the frontiers.

It was a time of continual wars and guerrilla raids,
and soon Jalalu'l Din's father was journeying westward
to avoid the horrors which lay in wait for Khorusan.
He made the pilgrimage to Mecca, settled briefly in
Damascus, and finally settled in Konya, then the flour-
ishing capital of the Western Seljuk Empire. Konya,
in central Turkey, preserves even today many of the
glorious buildings erected under the Seljuks. It was a
place where scholars and artists assembled, the seedbed
of the intellectual renaissance of the time. Here living
quietly and obscurely, learning at the feet of great mystical scholars, Jalalu'l Din seems to have spent the rest
of his life. In those days Asia Minor was known as Rum,
and so he is known to posterity as Rumi.

In time he became the leader of a mystical sect known
as the Mevlevi, who believed in cultivating a Platonic
type of mystical love, and in the benefits of music and

THE PERSIAN POETS

the dance. This sect still exists, and is well known today as the "dancing dervishes," their dance bearing a mystical reference to the movement of the spheres. Jalalu'l Din is perhaps the only great poet to have founded a religious order.

Essentially scholar and poet, he appears to have lived with one foot among his disciples, the other among his books and dreams. But the contemplative abbot was shaken to the depths at the age of thirty-seven when there suddenly appeared in Konya a weird figure known as Shamsi Tabriz, a young and incredibly handsome Persian, the son of a cloth merchant, who seemed in the abbot's eyes to possess a divine authority. For several months Jalalu'l Din spent his time closeted with this extraordinary youth. They became inseparable; and the monks of the Mevlevi sect began to complain openly because their beloved abbot no longer paid any attention to them. They resented the intruder and threatened violence against the young favorite who always wore a gown of coarse black felt and who was known as "the far-flying one" because he had journeyed widely. At last Shamsi Tabriz fled to Damascus. Jalalu'l Din sent his own son to bring the youth back. There was peace again, but only for a short while. Suddenly Shamsi Tabriz vanished. According to a story told some years later, he was set upon one night by seven conspirators, all heavily armed. Though without weapons, Shamsi Tabriz fought magnificently, escaped from them, left a few drops of blood on the earth, and vanished entirely from the world. In his honor, Jalalu'l Din, overcome by

THE SPLENDOR OF PERSIA

grief, wrote some of his greatest verses. One of these verses the poet Sa'di regarded as the greatest poem ever written in Persian:

> *Forever and ever the voice of love is calling.*
> *Our ship sails for Heaven: who are the voyagers*
> *Who have no desire to go with us?*
> *We have been in Heaven: we are companions of angels.*
> *So let us journey together, there is our country.*
> *We are even higher than angels and closer to Heaven.*
> *The end of our journey is a most perfect majesty.*

It is a note which we will hear again and again in the poetry of Jalalu'l Din. Heaven is close, almost we can breathe the scents flowing from it, almost we can rest in its pleasant shade:

> *Lovers, O lovers, it is time to abandon the world:*
> *The drum of departing is heard in my spiritual ears.*
> *Behold, the camel-driver is surely preparing his train:*
> *And shall we blame him when the travellers are asleep?*
> *Listen! The clanging of the camel-bells can be heard,*
> *And every moment a Soul is setting out to the frontier.*
> *From these inverted candles, from these blue awnings*
> *There comes a marvelous people, so that mysteries may*
> *be revealed.*
> *A heavy sleep falls from the circling spheres.*
> *Alas, that life should be like a feather and slumber so*
> *heavy.*
> *Dearest, seek the Beloved Friend: he is close by your side.*
> *Watchman, awake! Never should a watchman sleep.*

THE PERSIAN POETS

No poet ever spoke of the heavenly mysteries with more assurance or more grace. Like the great Andalusian poet who wrote in Arabic, Ibn Arabi, he speaks of Heaven as though he had been there and mapped out its pathways. So he says in one of the poems of his immense *Diwan:*

I have circled with the Nine Fathers in the Heavens,
For years I have followed the stars in their revolutions,
And always I was secret, dwelling in Him.
I touched the walls of the Kingdom, and my eyes were
open.
I received nourishment from God, as a child in the womb.
Men are born once: I was born many times.
And wearing a cloak of flesh, I have gone about spiritual
affairs,
But often I have slit my cloak wide open with my own
hands.
Long nights have I passed with the priests,
And I have slept with pagans in the market-places.
I am the green eyes of jealousy, the fever of sickness.
I am cloud and rain, I have swept down over the meadows.
Yet never did the dust of mortality touch the hem of my
garments.
I have watered a treasury of roses in the Field of Eternity.
I am not water or fire: I have no pride in me.
I am not fashioned of clay: I am the voice of mockery.
I am not Shamsi Tabriz: I am the pure Light!
Beware, if thou seest me! Tell no one I am here!

In this poem, where humility fights with pride, and

THE SPLENDOR OF PERSIA

the most assured wisdom is concealed in a cry of pain, Jalalu'l Din seems to be attempting to describe the heart of the mystery. Death was never far from his thoughts, and he was half in love with it. He wrote once:

> *Illness is a treasure, for it contains mercies:*
> *The kernel is soft when the rind is scraped away.*
> *O brother, the place of darkness and cold*
> *Is the fountain of life and the cup of ecstasy!*

Once, when he ordered music and dancing to accompany the funeral of one of his disciples, he was told that he was behaving improperly. "How should I do otherwise?" he said. "Surely when at last the spirit is freed from the dungeon of the body and wings its way to the source from which all things come, it is an occasion for rejoicing and for dancing."

Jalalu'l Din's greatest work was the *Mathnawi*, which he wrote at intervals over a period of forty-three years. In the six books which comprise this enormous work, he recounts all the legends, anecdotes, and histories of the Sufi faith that he can remember. Nothing is left out, and all is miracle. He called it "the path of the ascetics and the garden of the initiated," "the river of divine love" and "the mirror held up to the face of God." At once epic and textbook, the book claims to cover the entire field of love in all its multitudinous and divine aspects, and if it can be compared to any poem at all, it must be compared to Dante's *Paradiso*.

He died amid his beloved dervishes and was buried

close to the dancing floor, in the shadow of the Seljuk mosque erected for him. It was believed that power streamed from his grave, and in later years when the Ottoman Turks assumed power over a vast empire, the descendants of this Sufi poet were given the task of girding the sword of Osman on the Sultan. Konya became a place of pilgrimage: almost it was the spiritual centre of the Caliphate. By some strange twist of fate, a Persian mystical poet who died long before the Osmanli Turks conquered Constantinople was regarded as a kind of guardian angel to a despotic empire. During his life he was unkind to kings, calling them "dogs that bay at the moon." It is doubtful whether he would have rejoiced in the irony of his posthumous fame.

THE POET Sa'di was of a different temperament. Where Rumi is ecstatic, Sa'di clings to the earth, to love, to all human affairs, and has little interest in mystery. He tells the story that when he was a child, he was given to long vigils at night and earnest prayers on behalf of erring humanity. One night his father found him at his vigil and said: "You had better think more of your own sins than the sins of others—you won't find anyone so weak as you are, or so blind." The lesson struck home. Thereafter Sa'di no longer prayed for erring humanity. He observed them, laughed at them, occasionally delivered himself of sermons on a high didactic level, but even then, laughter came breaking through.

A small wiry man, with a fraying mustache and an air of bewilderment, he was confronted with crises all his life. His father, an official at the court of the Atabeg Sad ibn Zangi at Shiraz, died when Sa'di was a boy. Soon afterwards this boy was adopted by the Atabeg, whose name he took, and sent off to study at the Niza-miya College in Baghdad. These were violent times. The Mongol invasion occurred before he could return home. He wandered to India, where he visited the famous shrine of Siva. Then he went to Delhi, staying long enough to learn Hindustani. He wandered to Arabia, and seems to have settled down long enough to have a child by an Arabian girl. When the child died, he de-cided to drown his grief by undertaking an expedition to Abyssinia, and afterwards made pilgrimages to Mecca and Medina. For a while he lived in Damascus and Baal-bec, where he became a famous pulpit orator. Growing weary of civilization, he withdrew into the desert near Jerusalem, enjoying, like John the Baptist, the company of wild beasts, until, as he says, "the time came when some Franks took me prisoner and kept me with Jews in a trench at Tripoli, digging clay." We do not know the date; it may have been in 1229, when the Crusaders were wresting back from Saladin the territories they had lost. After countless hardships, a leading citizen of Aleppo chanced to see him working as a slave, had pity on him, ransomed him for ten dinars, offering a further hundred dinars if Sa'di would marry his daughter. Sa'di agreed, but soon wearied of his shrewish wife, divorced her, and went wandering through North Africa and

THE PERSIAN POETS

Asia Minor, never at peace with himself, a prey to tormenting thoughts, always moralizing. He was fifty when he returned to his native Shiraz. The Mongols had left the city undisturbed, and he was able to live quietly in the palace of his old patron's son, who had inherited the governorship of the province. There, except for frequent pilgrimages to Mecca, he remained until the end of his life, dying at the age of one hundred and seven, the longest lived and the most travelled of all the major poets of Persia.

Essentially, Sa'di is the moralizer and story-teller. All his poetry was written after his return to Shiraz: the work of an old man who lived on his memories and rejoiced in life and hated injustice. He wrote his famous *Gulistan*, or *Rose Garden*, in 1258, when he was seventy-four. It was the year when Hulagu Khan, with the Mongolian horde, swept down on Baghdad and in a week of terrifying slaughter, killed 800,000 people. The slaughter came to an end in the middle of February. In late spring, when the roses were dying, Sa'di was wandering in a rose garden with a friend, dismally aware of the impermanence of life, the horror of war, and all the other sorrows of the world. Gazing at the roses, Sa'di heard himself saying: "The rose has no permanence. It is better not to set the heart upon things which do not endure. And that is why it occurs to me to write a book on the rose garden, and I shall celebrate the roses, so that the chill winds of autumn cannot touch them." Then, as Sa'di relates the story, his friend flung the roses from his lap and clung to the skirt of the poet's

THE SPLENDOR OF PERSIA

robe and bade him fulfill his promise, saying: "When
the generous man maketh a promise, he keepeth it."
Sa'di thereupon set to work on the *Gulistan*, finishing
the book in a few days.

In this astonishing work, which has very little to do
with roses, written in prose, but with long sections in
verse, Sa'di tells stories about everything under the sun.
There are stories about kings and courtiers, dervishes
and beggars and courtesans and ordinary folk. Some are
brief, some long, but nearly all are pithy. Here are three
of his shorter stories:

> When one of the Kings of Khorusan saw his prede-
> cessor in a dream, his body no more than a mound of dust
> except for the two eyes which rolled and stared in their
> sockets, he asked the wise men the meaning of the dream.
> All of them failed to interpret the dream, except one soli-
> tary wise man who was possessed of understanding. And
> this wise man said: "He is saving his eyes so that he can
> look upon the present owner of the kingdom, and their
> rolling is the sign of his distress."

> An unjust King asked a wise man: "What is the
> greatest service I can offer God?" The wise man an-
> swered: "If Your Majesty would only fall asleep at
> noon." "What is the meaning of this?" the King asked.
> "I mean that there will be one moment at least when you
> do not oppress the people."

> One day when Nushirvan the Just was out hunting,
> and the game was being roasted, it was discovered there
> was no salt. A slave was sent to the village to get the salt.
> "And remember," said the King, "to pay a proper price

THE PERSIAN POETS

for it, otherwise the village will be ruined." The courtiers went up to the King and said: "How can it possibly ruin a village to take a little salt?" The King answered: "Tyranny always begins with small things. Those who come afterwards add a little each time, until it becomes a huge and monstrous thing."

Sa'di, with his rage against Kings and his continual moralizing, belonged to the people. He expressed platitudes gracefully, in stories and verses which were easily memorized. Though for a while he joined an order of Sufis, and wrote about them admiringly, he had little feeling for religion in its mystical aspects. Charming, tender, rooted to the earth, he delighted in the inconsistencies and oddities of people, and for this reason the Persians have always considered him among their greatest poets.

From his poems, we come to know Sa'di intimately, but no one ever claimed to know Mohammad Shabistari, the author of the *Gulshan i Raz*, or *Secret Rose Garden*, half as well. He was born near Tabriz about A.D. 1250. He joined an order of Sufis quite early in life and had a favorite disciple, Shaykh Ibrahim, and beyond this we know almost nothing about him. He wrote like an angel. Like Jalalu 'l Din, he was concerned to describe the spiritual raptures of the lover confronting the Beloved, who is the Face of God. For him embraces and kisses imply the lover's rapture when he comes close to God. Wine symbolizes spiritual knowledge, and the tavern the place where the lover is drunk with God. As he describes the Sufis in their

THE SPLENDOR OF PERSIA

ecstasies, he gives an impression of authority and clear, hard brightness. He writes like a man who has the glory of the Beloved continually in his gaze. Here are two poems, one describing Heavenly Beauty, the other the drunkenness of the Sufi as he approaches God:

I

From invisible worlds
Heavenly Beauty descends.
God hath planted her in our midst
Like a flag in the city,
And all the world trembles.
She rides upon a horse of comeliness
And flourishes her sword of eloquence.
All bow before her.
Saints and Kings, Sufis and Prophets
All surrender perpetually to her.

II

The angels are drunk with love: so is the soul.
The heavens are drunk, and so is the earth.
The sky quivers in the aroma of wine-fumes.
The angels, sipping pure wine out of wine-bowls,
Pour the dregs out on the world;
And from the scent men rise to heaven.
All the tipsy elements become fire and water.
And the frail little bodies of men frozen in ice
Are melted in the heat, becoming souls.
They thaw and become alive.
And everything in the world is drunken,

THE PERSIAN POETS

Forever straying from tavern to tavern.
Out of the wine-fumes emerges a philosopher,
Out of the color of wine emerges the story-teller.
From half a draught comes a saintly man,
From a full bowl comes a lover.
Still another swallows it all in one draught—
Goblet, tavern, cup-bearer, all the drunkards.
He swallows them all, and his mouth remains open!

Mohammad Shabastari employed the conventional Sufi symbolism, but he gave it fresh meaning and vivid color. The world is a flame, whirling up to God. Towards this flame the Sufis, drunk with love, reel in abandonment, unable to slake their thirst until they are bathed in the divine light, that glowing wine which is lit by the rays dancing from His face. "Beyond visions, beyond the dreaming of secret rooms, of lights and miracles, lies the Cup."

꙳ⵔꙮⵔꙮⵔꙮⵔꙮ

THERE WERE almost as many poets in Persia as in China: the names are legion, and it is impossible to discuss them all. But Hafiz—the name means "one who recites the Koran"—must not be omitted. He was the prince of Persian lyric poets, the most intoxicated of them all. He was born in Shiraz in 1320, spent most of his life there and died about 1390, being therefore a contemporary of Chaucer. There is this difference: no one now sings the songs of Chaucer, but Persian peasants can still recite the love-songs of Hafiz.

THE SPLENDOR OF PERSIA

We know almost nothing of his life except that he lived during a time of troubles, and served as court poet to a succession of minor princes ruling from Shiraz. He was often poor, and sometimes, as he remembered the ingratitude of princes, he showed a streak of bitterness. He had a huge thirst for wine, but he also thirsted after God—it is impossible at this late date to separate his drinking poems from his religious poems. "Drink deep, for the night comes," he wrote once, meaning perhaps that a man should drink both heavenly and earthly wines. It was characteristic of him that he should order these words to be written on his tombstone:

Though I am old, hold me all night in your arms,
So that at dawn, drunk with youth and fire, I arise.

There, once again and for the last time, he was employing his classic *double-entendre*, indicating God's mercy and the mercy of the beloved in the same breath.

He defies translation, and has been translated endlessly. The Victorians took him to their hearts, perhaps believing that his roses and nightingales were real roses and nightingales: it is possible that they were always heavenly ones, and certainly they were as stylized as the roses and nightingales which appear in Persian paintings and brocades. They forgot that he was obsessed with the splendor of God, but also with the terror which lies at the heart of things. Here he is singing sombrely:

Why drink alone? What's good in it?
Except that we are all drunkards together.

THE PERSIAN POETS

Unravel the knots of the heart, and leave
The heavenly spheres to unravel themselves.

The twists and turns of fortune—what of them?
This wheel has spun a thousand turns already.

Farhad dropped tears of blood for Shirin's lips,
Yet still the flowers are blossoming.

Surely the flowers are wise to fortune:
So clasp a flowering wine-glass till it fades.

Come, let us drink, let us go to ruin.
Sometimes under ruin one finds a treasure.

Like Hafiz drink your wine to the sound of harps:
The joy of the heart hangs on a silken string!

He is rarely so sombre. Often he is gay and frivolous: he laughs aloud, throws up his hands, roars with pleasure at the sight of the world around him—moonlight or sunset, the heaped pink roses of Shiraz filling the air with their scent, and the lovers walking under the trees. He approved of Noah, especially for his drunkenness. "Remember Noah," he wrote. "In the Ark he was no more than a speck of dust, and he cared nothing at all for the Deluge." He asked that wine be poured over his grave, and it amused him to think of his skull becoming a wine-cup. He played the game of *double-entendre* to the end, for when he died, people were still undecided about the meaning of his verses. Some even objected to his burial on consecrated ground. There was a dispute, and someone suggested the best solution was to use his works as

THE SPLENDOR OF PERSIA

an oracle. A copy of his poems was brought forward
and opened at random. They read:

> *May all of you accompany the coffin of Hafiz:*
> *Though deeply sinning, he will fly to Heaven.*

So Hafiz died in the midst of wars, gay, impenitent,
thirsting for God and writing poetry in the Sufi manner
to the end. Today he lies in a marble tomb shaped like
a garden pavilion, on a hillside overlooking Shiraz, the
biscuit-colored mountains behind, cypresses, roses, and
poppies all around. The texts of his poems decorate his
tomb. Visitors remove their shoes, for it is holy ground.

THE PERSIAN POETS

The Great Shahs

IN THE second half of the fifteenth century, Persia was divided among new rulers, the Turkomans in the west and the descendants of Tamerlane in the east. When the memory of the Great Conqueror grew dim, and his descendants were making their capitals on the borders of Persia at Herat and in Samarcand, far from

THE SPLENDOR OF PERSIA

the original centres of Persian power, there occurred once more the phenomenon which had occurred so often in Persian history. Once more there grew up in men's minds a hope for a purely Persian dynasty descended from the great Achaemenian Kings.

It was a time of war and great weariness. The Turkomans were divided into two families, the "Black Sheep" and the "White Sheep," who raided one another's territory and fought each other to a standstill. At this moment, an obscure tribesman from Azerbaijan, the leader of a small band of guerrilla soldiers known as the "Red Heads" defeated the Chief of the "White Sheep" and marched on Tabriz, where he crowned himself Shah in 1499. Western and central Persia fell to his soldiers. Only eastern Persia, now under the control of the Uzbeg Chieftain, Shaybani Khan, resisted. Suddenly the new Shah hurled his armies against the Uzbegs, who were lured into an ambush and cut down. The skull of Shaybani Khan, mounted on gold, was presented to the Shah to be used as a wine goblet.

No one has ever claimed such an august descent as the handsome young Emperor who crowned himself at Tabriz, for he claimed descent from the family of the Prophet Mohammad and from the ancient Achaemenian Kings, by way of the Sasanian King Yezdegerd, whose daughter was believed to have married Hussayn, the son of Ali. He was the sole survivor of a family which could trace its history to the seventh *Imam*, among whose descendants the most venerated was the saintly Shaykh Safi-u'-Din of Ardebil in northwest

THE GREAT SHAHS

Persia, who had died in 1334, but whose name was vividly remembered. Accordingly, the new Shah decreed that the dynasty should bear the name of Shaykh Safi and that all the Safavid Kings should be buried in the shrine of the Shaikh at Ardebil. For the first time in two and a half centuries, a purely Persian King was on the throne.

The creation of the new dynasty under Shah Ismail was greeted with wild enthusiasm. None of the previous conquerors except Hulagu had had the stuff of permanence. Wars had ravaged the country; there was a national desire for peace, and a need for a superbly gifted leader who could unite the country and restore the traditions of the race. Shah Ismail was a pious Shiite, an excellent soldier, and a superb administrator. The Venetian Angiolello, who visited him, remarked on his graceful demeanor and physical strength. "He is fair, handsome, and pleasing," said the Venetian. "He is not tall, but of a light and well-built appearance. His hair is reddish, and he wears mustachios. He is as brave as a gamecock and stronger than any of his lords."

Shah Ismail had need to be brave, for it was his misfortune to come to the throne when the bigoted and bloodthirsty Sultan Selim I was on the throne of Turkey. Selim was in no mood to tolerate a heretic as a neighbor. He was the greatest soldier of the House of Othman, and the most determined to inherit the Caliphate. When Shah Ismail swept down on Baghdad and desecrated some of the tombs of the Sunni saints and put Sunni mullahs to death, Selim swore revenge. His first step was to put to death some 40,000 of his own people, believing or pretending to believe they were heretics. Then he marched against Persia.

Shah Ismail was unprepared. His small army was confronted with the largest army of the time, composed of cavalry and artillery divisions and the famous Janissaries, his relentless guardsmen, all of them Christians, forming a foreign legion of musketeers at the service of the Turkish Sultan. Against them Shah Ismail could only set his tribesmen who served under their own chiefs yet owed fanatical loyalty to their sovereign. They worshipped Ismail as a saint, and some even refused to wear armor in battle, believing they were sufficiently protected by the presence of the Shah. When the armies met, Shah Ismail attacked on both flanks of the Turkish forces: he hoped to win by a swift, sharp attack. Instead, his soldiers were mowed down by the musket-fire of the Janissaries. The Shah killed the commander of the Janissaries but was himself badly wounded. He was forced to leave the battlefield. Thereupon his followers fled the field, and Selim gave orders that all the male prisoners should be massacred. It was a great victory for Selim. To crown the victory, he marched on Tabriz, which immediately surrendered. It was said of Shah Ismail that after his defeat he never smiled again. He died in 1524 at Ardebil, bitterly mourned by his people.

꠹꠹꠹꠹꠹꠹

His ELDEST son, Tahmasp, came to the throne when he was still a child. He grew up to be even

THE GREAT SHAHS

more fanatical than his father, and he lacked Ismail's saving grace of kindness. He was slight and slender, with a dark face, thick lips, and a repellent beard, but he possessed exquisite taste and some of the best Safavid carpets come from the court looms of his time. As he grew older, he grew more cautious. Selim had died, to be replaced by Sulayman the Magnificent, who was to boast that he was master of many kingdoms, the ruler of three continents, and the lord of two seas. From his father, Sulayman had inherited a full treasury, a well-equipped army, and a desire for conquest. All the Barbary Coast, all of Syria and Asia Minor and Rumania were in his hands: he conquered Budapest. When he decided to attack Persia, it was almost an afterthought. He seems to have decided upon the conquest because there was nothing for his Janissaries to do. He led his armies to north Persia, hoping a show of force would make Shah Tahmasp surrender. The Persians simply withdrew. It was November and the rain falling in the passes was freezing into ice. Sulayman, determined to punish them, brought the army through the defiles of the Zagros Mountains. Swollen streams swept part of the artillery away. Hundreds of animals had to be abandoned. Gun carriages had to be burnt, to prevent them from falling into the hands of the enemy. Cannon were spiked and buried underground. In despair, Sulayman ordered the army to turn west, and when the hills of Luristan fell away and the plains of Mesopotamia lay before him, he sighed with relief. He had been defeated, not by the Persian army, but by the misery of a Persian winter.

THE SPLENDOR OF PERSIA

The Persians were under no illusions about the strength of the magnificent Sulayman. They held their breaths, waiting for the next onslaught, which came four years later. Then once again Tabriz was taken by the enemy, and Shah Tahmasp showed his incapacity as a military leader. It was said that for eleven years afterwards he refused to leave his palace, for fear of assassination. In 1559, Bayazid, the son of Sulayman, rebelled against his father and took refuge in the Persian court, bringing his four sons with him. Anyone who knew the character of Shah Tahmasp might have guessed what would happen. The Shah promised to safeguard the rebel's life. At the same time, he sent messages to the Sultan. A little more than a year later, Bayazid and his four sons were treacherously surrendered to the Sultan in exchange for 400,000 pieces of gold. Then in Constantinople they were publicly executed.

None of the foreigners who came to the Persian court have a good word to say for the Shah. Grim-faced, earnest, with a fiery temper and a strange habit of pulling endlessly on his beard, Tahmasp was the soul of treachery. Fear drove him half-insane. When the English adventurer Antony Jenkinson made the long voyage which brought him down the Volga and over the Caspian Sea to the Persian Court and presented the letters of Queen Elizabeth to the mad King, he replied: "O thou unbeliever, we have no need to be friends with unbelievers!" Tahmasp, who was then attempting to draw up a peace treaty with Sulayman, carefully considered the advantages to be gained by sending Jenkin-

THE GREAT SHAHS

son's head to the Sultan, as a friendly gesture. Later, he decided there were advantages in trading with England. Jenkinson returned to London with gifts for the Queen and good profits to show for his adventure.

Shah Tahmasp's reign, which lasted fifty-two years, brought little glory to Persia but it offered a breathing-space for artists. There were long intervals of peace. Fanaticism lessened, and artists flourished. The finest Persian carpets date from this time. Already there was emerging the style, at once graceful and vivid, which was to come to full maturity in the reign of Shah Abbas I, the greatest of the Safavid Emperors, whose fine clear-cut features and brilliance in war contrast oddly with the petulant ugliness and cowardice of his predecessor.

⟡⟡⟡⟡⟡⟡⟡⟡

SHAH ABBAS rejoiced in being King. He came to the throne after a short period of confusion, during which three Kings were crowned. He was only sixteen or seventeen when he was proclaimed Shah, but he was quick-witted and knew exactly what was demanded of him. Small, handsome, and well-proportioned, with a dark complexion like a Spaniard—Sir Anthony Sherley said of him that he possessed "a manlike blacknesse"—he showed throughout his long reign that he was the complete master of his country and feared no enemies beyond the borders. He had a huge army. He could muster 300,000 horsemen and 70,000 musketeers. He liked war and was fearless in battle, and he enjoyed the arts of peace. His first task was to make a

THE SPLENDOR OF PERSIA

treaty of peace with the Turks; his second to destroy the Uzbegs who had captured the sacred city of Meshed, which contains the shrine of the Imam Reza, the eighth of the twelve Imams in line of succession after Ali. He punished the Uzbegs so mercilessly that they never again in his lifetime attacked the city. When he rode away in triumph, he ordered his soldiers to stick the heads of Uzbegs on their lances. When the two English adventurers, Sir Anthony and Sir Robert Sherley, saw Shah Abbas for the first time, it was dusk and the King was riding at the head of his victorious army. At first the Englishmen could not make out the strange objects on the lances. A great barbaric procession was winding past them. Women were running beside the soldiers. Everyone was laughing. Wine was flowing. It was like the sudden onrush of a horde which had come out of Central Asia: deafening noise, clashing of spears, wild laughter. Suddenly Shah Abbas rode up to where the two Englishmen were standing. The Shah was drunk with triumph. He smiled, turned to the Englishmen, complimented them on their presence on this auspicious occasion, and kissed them. The barbarian who had massacred the Uzbegs showed himself to be the most charming and civilized of men.

There was little peace for the Sherleys for weeks afterwards. Nearly every night the Shah entertained them, gave them presents, poured honors on them. They were given high rank. At table they were seated beside the Shah, who was genuinely fond of them, but was chiefly impressed with their knowledge of western armaments. The Englishmen had brought a cannon-founder with them. And the Shah, who realized he might soon have to meet a powerful Turkish army, set the Sherleys and the cannon-founder to work.

Sulayman the Magnificent was dead, and the Turkish Empire was being ruled by an impatient grandson devoted to the arts of war and determined to put a stop to the growing power of Persia. The battle was fought on the banks of Lake Urmiya. Instead of charging the Turkish flanks, like Shah Tahmasp, Shah Abbas sent part of his army behind the Turkish forces, and cunningly hid his main forces. The Turks, thinking the forces behind them belonged to the main body of the Persian army, countermarched and prepared to annihilate the small diversionary force. They were too late. Suddenly Shah Abbas unloosed his most highly trained troops at the enemy. His cannon barked. The Turks were routed. When the battle was over, 20,000 Turkish heads were heaped up outside the royal tents of Shah Abbas, and the remnants of the Sultan's army were in full flight.

For the first time, the Persians had won a victory over the Turks. The fruits of the victory were the lost provinces of Persia. Purchas, who was a friend of Robert Sherley, described the results of the battle: "The mighty Ottoman, terror of the Christian world, quaketh of a Sherley-fever, and gives hopes of approaching fates. The prevailing Persian has learned Sherleian arts of war, and he which before knew not the use of ordnance, hath now 500 pieces of brass. Hence hath the present Abbas

won from the Turk seven great Provinces, from Derbent to Bagdat."

Shah Abbas reigned for forty-two years, but he was
never again to enjoy a victory as great as this. It was
the turning-point of his life, and the turning-point of
Persian history. Henceforward there was to be peace
in Persia until his death. Not since Darius and Shapur
had there been a Shah on the throne so determined to
rule beneficently.

He could be cruel, but he nearly always kept his
ferocity in check. He could make sudden arbitrary
judgments, but that is one of the privileges of Kingship.
He was fanatical in his worship of the Imam Reza, and
twice walked the entire distance of 800 miles from his
new capital in Isfahan to the city of Meshed to pay
tribute at the shrine of the dead Imam. He made pilgrimages fashionable, and in so doing knit the country together, for the pilgrimages became part of the official
worship within the empire. But his most enduring gift
to Persia lay in the arts of painting, carpet-making,
and building. He encouraged artists and treated them
reverently. He had removed his capital to Isfahan in
1598. Thereafter Isfahan became the most beautiful
capital in the world.

꜀꜀꜀꜀꜀꜀꜀

WHEN Isfahan was at the height of its importance and prestige, it was larger than Paris. It was
said to have 600,000 people, 162 mosques, 48 religious

THE GREAT SHAHS

colleges, 1,802 caravanserais, and 273 public baths. It was so magnificent that the Persians coined the saying: "Isfahan is half the world"—*Isfahan nisf-i-jahan.* Though much of the glory has departed, enough remains to take one's breath away.

Viewed from the air, it seems no more than a small oasis. The desert rings it round. Bare rugged mountains —one of them, shaped like a sleeping girl, appears in countless miniatures of the time—lie close to the city. A traveller coming by airplane sees a mass of chennar trees with the blue domes of occasional mosques peering among them. You tell yourself this is a city like twenty other Persian cities: dusty roads, a few fountains, the dark-robed women wandering through the bazaars. Here and there you come upon brilliantly tiled mosques, but it is not until you reach the great *Maidan-i-Shah* (the parade-ground of the Shah) that you realize the full perfection of the place. This parade-ground is a thing of extreme and exquisite beauty, perhaps the most beautiful place on earth. Here are palaces and mosques and bazaars displayed beside a great sandy square, all glittering, all on fire with jewelled colors; and the eye, searching for a place to rest, goes from amazement to amazement.

When the jeweller Tavernier came to Isfahan, he noted that the Maidan was surrounded with the arcades for dancing-girls, and a great tree rose in the centre of the square. From the topmost branch of the tree hung a gold cup. The officers of the court amused themselves by riding on ponies past the tree, then turning on their saddles and attempting to shoot down the cup with

THE SPLENDOR OF PERSIA

bows and arrows. The parade-ground in those days was a polo field, a place where soldiers were drilled and games were played, and it was also the King's garden. Some days it was transformed into a market-place. Here came sellers of tiger-skins from Nishapur and Hyrcania; leather saddles, jewelled ornaments, bales of silk cloth from China. At night it was illuminated by hanging lanterns. Here gallants from the Court rubbed shoulders with beggars, and the Shah himself looked down from his high palace at the gay throngs below.

But though that immense parade-ground possessed an importance of its own, the decoration surrounding it has a still greater importance. Here, at the order of Shah Abbas, the most beautiful of all mosques was built. It is called simply the Masjid-i-Shah, the mosque of the Shah. The dome is the blue of diamonds, and the yellow of sunflowers. It rises high, dominating the parade-ground, and seems never to be still, so delicate it is. A superb, effortless power seems to emanate from it. It lies behind two high arched portals, one set at an angle to the other, and somehow this strange, slanted entrance to the mosque acquires the appearance of improvization: a dome at once so august and so gentle should not, one thinks, be so capriciously placed. It seems not to have been made by the hands of man. It flowers effortlessly. As you approach closer, its sheer immensity baffles. Even in the cavernous interior, where the walls are filled with many-colored faience, you are aware of an effortless flowering. There is nothing stern here. Joyfully, as though overwhelmed by the beauty they saw around

THE GREAT SHAHS

them, the architects of Shah Abbas built a mosque
proclaiming the joy of God, whose name in Kufic inscriptions is endlessly written on the colored walls.

The Mosque of the Shah is only the beginning. The
small and still more delicate Mosque of Shaykh Lutfullah, which faces the royal palace of Shah Abbas, is
even more marvellous. The blue-and-yellow dome somehow suggests the perfection of a field in paradise. It is
more stately than the dome of the Mosque of the Shah,
and shines with a calmer light, passionless, with a hint
of austerity; and when you enter the dome-chamber,
you are made aware of such a wealth of decoration,
so many twined flowers, so many gleaming inscriptions,
that the mind reels. It is like entering a treasure-chest,
but one which does not lead you to desire the treasure
so abundantly displayed: it is enough that it is there.
The color of the glaze is of sun-dried blue grapes when
the sun's shadow falls on them. Everything in the interior suggests peace, maturity, and quietness. If one
were to suggest the two most superb gifts which Persia
has given to the world, almost inevitably one would
have to choose the Persepolis stairway and the Mosque
of Shaykh Lutfullah.

There is no end to the treasures around the parade-
ground. The royal palace, known as Ali Qapu, combines
delicacy and strength in a way which is almost too
obvious. Above the heavy brick archway, slender
wooden columns arise, forming a kind of roof patio,
but the columns are so wonderfully shaped and so intimately related to the surrounding minarets of the

THE SPLENDOR OF PERSIA

mosques, that everything about the palace appears inevitable and at the same time, it seems about to float
away into thin air. On the patio, the Emperor held
audiences, and from the balcony, he looked down at the
games and processions and markets below. Here, sitting
cross-legged on a low-lying couch of gold, he received
ambassadors and administered his empire. Here the
dancing-girls danced at night with oil-lamps in their
hands, the harpists played, and the wine flowed freely.
Thomas Herbert speaks of "the Ganimed boys in vests
of cloth of gold, rich spangled Turbants, and embroidered sandals, curled hair dangling over their
shoulders, with rolling eyes and vermilion cheeks, carrying in their hands flagons of best Metal; and they went
up and down, profferring the delight of Bacchus to
such as were disposed to take it."

Behind the patio, entered once again by an immense
archway, lies the palace proper, where all the rooms are
painted with hunting scenes and with lovers wandering
hand-in-hand through Persian gardens. There is hardly
a square inch of those walls which is not painted over
by a superb artist in love with the gaiety of life. In the
carved niches, where the wine-flagons were kept, there
are paintings; lovers wander about the roofs and lie in
wait for you in hidden corners. The smell of wine still
lingers here. Thomas Herbert said the parade-ground
was "the most Aromatick place in the whole universe,"
but it is likely that the palace was the most heavily
scented, as it was the gayest, the noisiest, and the most
tumultuous building on that immense square.

THE GREAT SHAHS

There is still one further treasure to be mentioned—
the Chihil Situn, or Hall of Forty Columns, where
Shah Abbas was accustomed to hold court beside a lotus-
pond. And once again we find the walls painted with
the gentle, laughing cavaliers escorting their young
women in Persian gardens. Once again stateliness and
immense dignity are combined with grace. In the honey-
scented garden the red-painted columns rise perhaps
fifty feet high. A thousand people could be gathered in
the portico, and there would be room for more. And
yet this vast palace does not suggest power. It suggests a
power so assured of itself that it has no need to demonstrate itself.

Isfahan remains a monument to the early Safavid
Emperors. From Shah Ismail to Shah Abbas, progress
in the arts was swift, steady, and assured. We see it in
the wonderful mosques, but it is no less visible in the
paintings and the carpets. If you look at a painting by
Bihzad, who was a contemporary of Shah Ismail, or by
Riza Abbasi, who was a contemporary of Shah Abbas,
you see the same delicacy, the same strength, the same
joy in life, the same absolute serenity in the face of the
future which was to prove so tragically insecure.

The Persian painting of this time followed conven-
tions foreign to western painting. Like the Chinese, they
painted without shadows. In the hunting scenes, rocks
are mauve or purple, the poplars stand perfectly still in
the windless afternoon and wisps of white cloud float
unhurriedly across the turquoise air. Lovers kneel
beneath cherry trees, holding hands, elegant even in their

THE SPLENDOR OF PERSIA

raptures. Imperial portraits, lovers, the hunt—there is almost nothing else. Occasionally, we come upon heroic scenes, the heroes grappling with dragons, Mohammad flying on his woman-headed horse Buraq into the Seventh Heaven, whole armies on the field of battle; but everything is stylized and there is never any effort to paint according to the laws of perspective. In their grace and immobility, the people who peer out at us from Persian paintings resemble the people we see in the great mosaics of Italy: they are not of this world, but belong to a world where everything is calm and beautiful, intelligible and serene, where anger is unknown and all desires are sated. Nearly every Persian painting is a kind of portrait of paradise.

A Persian carpet is a more deliberate portrait of paradise, with its running streams and singing birds and shady trees. Even the prayer-rugs are pictures of gardens, though sometimes the tree depicted on them is the Tree of Life, a symbol as old as Persia herself. But all is stylized, deliberately removed from the immediate world of the senses to a mysterious other-world, where there is no passing of time and no sunset: an eternal noontime. Look carefully at a Persian carpet: you will see pathways, clumps of flowers, nests of singing birds, strange, curling shapes which reveal themselves to be lions or panthers or verses of the Koran or the name of God Himself. What is most remarkable about the carpets of the period of the Safavid Emperors is their brilliance of coloring, their boldness, and the resourcefulness of the artists who designed them in making the

THE GREAT SHAHS

parts subservient to the total design. The Ardebil carpet, which hangs in the Victoria and Albert Museum, paints a garden in spring-time with huge sprays of blossoms and innumerable animals wandering among the flowering trees. At the centre, a great yellow sun symbolizes the majesty of God. On either side, as though falling from the yellow centre, are two delicately fashioned mosque-lamps. The glory of God, mosque-lamps, a garden—one might have thought it impossible to represent those three things in a single carpet, yet it has been done superbly. For the Persians, as for the Arabs, a carpet nearly always possesses a religious significance. So on the famous Ardebil carpet we find the words:

I HAVE NO REFUGE IN THE WORLD OTHER THAN THY THRESHOLD,
MY HEAD HAS NO PROTECTION OTHER THAN THY PORCHWAY.

A deeply religious feeling informed the early Safavid Emperors. With their joy in life went a sense of absolute devotion to God and to Mohammad, the Prophet of God. Outside the Mosque of the Shah there used to hang on ceremonial occasions the blood-stained shirt reputed to have been worn by the martyr Hussayn, the grandson of the Prophet. Within the Mosque was the Koran supposed to have been written by the hand of the sainted Imam Reza, whose shrine was at Meshed. It was characteristic of Shah Abbas that he should have built his palace in the midst of a forest of superbly decorated mosques.

THE SPLENDOR OF PERSIA

For over a century, until the death of Shah Abbas at a ripe age in 1628, Persia went from one triumph to another. During the reigns of three Emperors, long periods of internal peace permitted artists to create works of enduring power. In miniatures, in painting, in architecture they excelled themselves and rose to heights they never reached again.

When Shah Abbas died, the long years of peace came to an end, and the nightmare began.

THE GREAT SHAHS

The Awakening

THE STORY of modern Persia since the time of Shah Abbas is one of slow decay, followed by a magnificent awakening. For centuries, Persia seemed to be living in a dream of mediaevalism. New dynasties arose, Shah followed Shah, the aimless progress of half-mad rulers led the country to the brink of annihilation. Then by a lucky chance, or by one of those alterations in the course of history which have happened too often in Persia not to be due to some profound characteristic of the Persian spirit, a new dynasty arose which threw off the weight of the nightmare. Almost overnight, Persia became a modern state.

After the death of Shah Abbas the line of the Safavid Emperors flickered out like candles. Shah Safi (1629-1642) was a bloodthirsty tyrant who put the princes of the blood to death and killed off most of the generals and councillors who had attended upon his grandfather. Shah Abbas won battles; Shah Safi lost them. The Sultan Murad IV repeatedly invaded the country. Hamadan, Kazvin, and Baghdad all fell before the Turks. Murad IV exceeded even Shah Safi in his thirst for blood-letting. It was said of him that he tolerated no crimes but his own. For thirty-nine days Baghdad held out against the Turks, the Sultan commanding his troops in person, wearing chain-mail and an immense turban with a jeweled aigrette. On the fortieth day, the order for the final assault was given. According to a contemporary chronicler, the Turks rushed in, "so hot upon slaying and plundering that they killed all they met, the whole night that this sacking lasted. In short there were in Bagdat One and thirty thousand pick'd and choice Soldiers, and twenty thousand Volunteers, all whom we have put to sword, not having one escaped to carry the news to the other Towns of Persia."

Shah Safi was close at hand with a large Persian force, but he did nothing to save the city. He died four

THE AWAKENING

years later, satisfied to have outlasted the Sultan by two years, though he died as miserably as the bloodthirsty tyrant he opposed and from the same cause—both drank themselves to death.

Shah Abbas II was a nonentity, and Shah Sulayman was a cruel and bloodthirsty tyrant who appeared to model himself upon Sultan Murad IV. Krusinski, the Jesuit priest who was living in Isfahan, said of him that "when he was in wine, no one about him was sure of his life or estate. He caused hands, feet, nose, and ears to be cut off, eyes to be plucked, and lives to be sacrificed at the least whim." When courtiers left his presence they felt their heads to be sure they were still on their shoulders. It was a time of pomp and pageantry, of vast intrigues, and endless murders. In the paintings of the artists of this time there is a strange woodenness, a curious uneasiness, as though the world, which had seemed so exciting and breathlessly beautiful in the time of Shah Abbas I, had suddenly grown dim.

When Shah Sultan Hussayn ascended the throne in 1694, the vitality of the Safavids was already ebbing away. Hussayn detested killing, and it is possible that he also detested being Shah. A weak, childish simpleton completely under the influence of the mullahs, he followed at all times the pattern of a pious ruler determined upon peace at all costs. To maintain the peace, he offered bribes to the tribesmen on the frontiers. In 1722 the storm broke. The Afghans, barely 20,000 strong, advanced on Isfahan. They had 100 swivel guns with 2-pound balls. They reached a village some 11 miles from

Isfahan and came in sight of a Persian army of 50,000 men with 29 heavy guns. The Persian right wing charged and broke through the enemy lines, but when the left wing charged, the Afghans held firm. They knew the weakness and lack of organization of the Persians; and when they found the Persian artillery unprotected, they surrounded the gunners, cut them down, and turned the guns on the Persians, especially on the cavalry which had become completely panic-stricken. Then the Afghans surrounded the city and starved the inhabitants into surrender. The Shah was captured and brought into the presence of the Afghan conqueror, humbling himself and saying: "Since the great Sovereign of the Universe does not will that I shall reign any longer, I resign the Empire to thee." For seven more years he was allowed to live on, enclosed within a palace, then he was quietly put to death. The great empire of the Safavids was at an end, though Tahmasp, the son of Shah Hussayn lived on and organized rebellions.

The most rebellious and the most deeply religious of the Persian provinces has always been Khorusan. From this province had come the armed bands which a thousand years before had toppled the Ommayad Caliph from his throne. Out of Khorusan came the impulse to throw out the detested Afghans. At the head of the rebel army was an Afshar tribesman, Nadir Kuli, who was destined to restore the prestige of Persia. Once again, out of obscurity came a compelling figure able to weld the Persians together after years of defeat.

THE AWAKENING

In his youth, Nadir earned a poor living making sheepskin coats and keeping goats. Born in a wayside tent, and soon left fatherless, he was carried off in a raid by Uzbeg tribesmen when he was eighteen. The boy and his mother were sold as slaves. Four years later, his mother dead, Nadir succeeded in escaping and entering the service of the governor of Abivard. He was handsome and showed himself to advantage in the small court of the governor. He had a long face, his underlip jutted out a little, and his voice was thick, but the face was well-made; his large, black eyes were particularly fine and he was six feet tall. He asked for the hand of the governor's daughter and married her. On her father's death he became governor. He was lord over a hundred small villages, and thirsted for power. The Viceroy of Khorusan, a certain Malik Mahmud who ruled from Meshed, summoned him to court. On the way, Nadir defeated an army of Uzbeg tribesmen, the same group of Uzbegs which had captured him and sold him into slavery, and he gave a full account of his adventures to Malik Khan, perhaps exaggerating them, for he was not believed at court and instead of being rewarded he was punished with a beating. He turned robber and at the head of a pathetically small band of outlaws captured Nishapur in the name of Shah Tahmasp, the pretender to the throne. Then, one by one, he defeated Afghan and Turkish armies, and pushed the Russians out of the Caspian provinces where they were busily extending their influence. A few years later, when Russia and Turkey were at war, Nadir occupied

THE SPLENDOR OF PERSIA

Baku and Derbent, threatening to join the Turks against Peter the Great unless the lost Caspian provinces were returned to him. He had thrown Afghans, Turks, and Russians out of Persia, and a grateful assembly of nobles elected him Shah.

Young and vigorous, with a taste for adventure, Nadir Shah had no intention of standing still. In sixteen incredible years he captured Kandahar, Kabul, Delhi, Bokhara, Mosul, and Basra. By the end of his reign, the Persian Empire stretched from the Indus to the Caucasus. He had Napoleon's gift for quick movement and lightning decisions, and, like Napoleon, he was to taste the bitterness of victory.

It was the time when the great Mughal Empire in India, once ruled by Shah Jehan, was in full decay under Mohammad Shah, "a man never without a woman in his arms and a goblet of wine in his hands." Mohammad Shah sold high offices to the highest bidder, wrote execrable poetry, and seems to have been incapable of organizing any resistance against the enemies in his midst or on the frontiers. When Nadir Shah laid siege to Kandahar, Mohammad Shah left the city to its own fate, sending no reinforcements; and when, after a year's siege, Kandahar fell, he made no attempt to block the progress of the Persian armies. Kabul, the main land-gate to India, fell soon afterwards. Then Nadir Shah struck with the suddenness of a thunderstorm, marched straight on Delhi and met the huge Indian army at Karnal, some sixty miles to the north of Delhi on the right bank of the Jumna River. Mo-

THE AWAKENING

hammad Shah seems to have thought the Persians would simply break their strength against the great wall of his massed soldiers, his elephants, and his heavy artillery. Too late he realized that Nadir Shah aimed at the destruction of his dynasty and the capture of all the treasuries of India. To the invader, as one Moslem King speaking to another, he sent a message, begging for an armistice and received the chilling reply: "I am no emissary of mercy, but one of those scourges sent by God to punish the wickedness of nations."

Quietly, with amazing vigor, Nadir Shah set about reducing the vast Indian army to impotence. There were skirmishes, ambushes, a whole series of short concerted actions. His aim was to madden the Indian troops into surrender. He captured part of the Indian artillery, and then he began to bombard the Indian camp. There was no battle, only a series of brief engagements, and when Mohammad Shah ordered his soldiers to attack, they refused. In despair, the degenerate descendant of the Mughals surrendered. The victor marched in triumph to Delhi, which he stripped bare, collecting all the spoils of the palaces including the famous Peacock Throne and the Koh-i-Nor diamond. His booty was valued at $300,000,000. Not content with the booty, he massacred the people of Delhi and then, having restored Mohammad Shah to the throne—it was impossible to believe that this unwarlike prince would ever be dangerous—he marched back to Persia. Altogether, he had spent just two months in India. Never

THE SPLENDOR OF PERSIA

before or afterwards had a great empire been so swiftly brought to its knees.

If he had been a different kind of man, Nadir Shah might have brought strength and prosperity to Persia. He had a keen intelligence, and a keener delight in conquest for the sake of loot, but he had no conception of government. Once he was discussing the delights of Paradise with a holy man. Suddenly he shouted: "Is there war in Paradise, and can one slay an enemy there?" And when he was told that wars were no longer practicable in Paradise, he swore he had no desire to go there. "I must die in war," he said, and remained, though the King of a vast empire, something of a bandit chieftain to the end.

When he led his armies back to Persia, he left behind him a smoke-blackened trail of burning villages and despairing peasants. Yet he was in no mood for rest. He swung north, captured Bokhara and Khiva, releasing thousands of Persian and Russian slaves of these emirates. The following year he attacked the tribesmen of Daghestan, who had killed his only brother, but when they retreated into the dense forests, he was baffled and could not follow them. Then, for the rest of his short reign, he seems to have fed on frustration, hating everyone around him, even his own sons, playing the game of murder as he set one courtier against another. He was growing old quickly. His health was bad, he suffered from jaundice and his teeth fell out: like Napoleon III, he employed cosmetics and dyed his

THE AWAKENING

beard. For some reason he suddenly turned against the entire Shia sect which comprised most of the population of Persia and ordered them to substitute the Imam Ja'afar for Ali, the patron saint of Persia. The Persians rebelled, and the Turks, determined to put down a new heresy, sent a huge army against him. Once again Nadir Shah showed his military genius, employing the same ruse as before, capturing the enemy's artillery and then surrounding them. It was his last victory. Thereafter he abandoned his attempt to change the religion of the Persians and settled down to count the great hoards of loot acquired in his wars. He became a miser, distressed whenever he discovered that a single unnecessary *dirhem* had been expended by the state. As always he set his officers against each other, thinking to obtain peace among them by balancing their enmities. One night his own bodyguard decided to put an end to him. Hopelessly outnumbered, he met his death fighting bitterly to the end. He had reigned for only twelve years.

Nadir Shah was a phenomenon. No one quite like him had ever appeared in Persia. He was not a Persian, but a Turkoman, and he had no particular love for the Persians whom he used as instruments for his own aggrandizement. He seems to have spoken Persian with difficulty, and usually talked in Turki. Yet the Persians were compelled to regard him as an almost sacred figure: there was magic in his victories. They followed him because he fulfilled their idea of kingship; and because he was universally successful in war, they even

THE SPLENDOR OF PERSIA

forgave him for putting out the eyes of his own son.
To the end, he was a man of superb physique, with a
voice like thunder and a terrible intensity of gaze. He
said once that of all things he liked most the melons of
Herat, and after this a good horse. He was the last of
the conquering Persian Kings, and with his death in
1747, the story of the Persian empire comes to an end.
Never again was Persia to extend over so great a territory.

When he died, the empire broke apart. An Afghan
general ruled over the northern province of Azerbaijan,
Khorusan fell to the hands of Nadir Shah's blind
nephew, Shah Rukh, and the southern province of
Fars obeyed a certain Karim Khan, a poor soldier of
saintly character who was an excellent administrator,
ruling from the city of Shiraz which he made beautiful.
Once again, as so often before, Persia had changed almost overnight from being a vast empire to being a
number of small feudal states quarrelling with one another. And once again there emerged a genius to weld
the nation together.

THERE WAS NOTHING in the appearance of
Aga Mohammad to suggest an Emperor. On his beard-
less and shrivelled face there was always a look of surprise. At the age of five, he had been castrated; he had all
the faults of an eunuch to the end. He was crafty, mis-
chievous, and cruel. He had a passion for jewels, which
he hoarded. He tolerated no opposition. He was the

THE AWAKENING

chief of the Qajar tribe, and his dynasty was to rule until 1923.

As chief of a tribe, Aga Mohammad possessed a small standing army. With this he went out to conquer first Georgia, and then the province of Khorusan. After a forced march, he threw his army against Tiflis, where he massacred the priests and the infirm, and enslaved the rest of the population. He was a man who made lightning decisions and gloried in warfare. Having brought Tiflis under his control, he marched against Khorusan, ruled by the blind King, Shah Rukh. He had no difficulty in winning the province by force of arms, but he had more difficulty in making Shah Rukh reveal the hinding place of his jewels. In the end he decided to set his torturers to work. One by one, Shah Rukh revealed where he had hidden the jewels. In the end even the famous ruby of Aurengzeb, part of the spoils of Nadir Shah's invasion of India, was surrendered. Aga Mohammad showed no mercy, watched the torture, and grimaced with pleasure after each jewel was discovered. A few days later, the unhappy Shah Rukh died, his last words a curse on the eunuch who had destroyed him.

Aga Mohammad destroyed everything he touched: no Persian ruler before or since ever possessed such a talent for pure evil. He was detested by his closest acquaintances and feared by everybody. Yet he possessed immense physical courage and was perfectly certain he could claim moral ascendancy on everyone who came within the influence of the throne. He found two body-guards quarrelling. Incensed by their behavior, he ordered that they should be executed the next morning and it amused him to keep them in his service during the evening before the execution. Quite deliberately, knowing exactly what he was doing, he behaved towards them as though there had been no threat of execution. They attended to him and saw to his comforts. He smiled at them pleasantly, his lips curling. Then, still feeling immeasurably superior to his doomed body-guard, he went to sleep. At some time during the night the body-guards murdered him. He had reigned for no more than three years, and on every one of those thousand days he had committed crimes.

He was succeeded by his nephew, Fath Ali Shah, who was tall, handsome, violently energetic, and three-quarters mad. The new King shared with his uncle an inordinate love for jewelry, and spent long hours in his treasury counting his collection. He had a long, black, silky beard which reached below his waist. He dressed magnificently. He was proud of his vast number of children. He was the first of the Persian Kings to feel the full weight of western penetration and envelopment. He came to the throne in 1797. It was the time of the French Revolution and of tremendous upheavals. The Shah still lived as though he were a reigning monarch of the Middle Ages. With his gown of gold tissue, his ropes of pearls, and his immense crown with the sweeping aigrette, he resembled someone who had strayed out of another age; and when the Russians annexed Georgia, he was incapable of leading his armies

THE AWAKENING

against them. Once when he was violently annoyed by the behavior of the Russians, he summoned the ambassador to his court. He was wearing his "robe of wrath" of bright crimson, and carried a ruby-hilted dagger at the waist. He frowned upon the Russians, ordered them to return Georgia to Persia, and threatened dire punishments, regarding himself as "the lord of terrible aspect" whose slightest whisper must be obeyed. The Russians went on with their plans for annexing the rest of Persia.

The nineteenth century was a century of foreign invasions. Russians, Germans, and British fought for mastery over the land. The long reign of the mad Fath Ali Shah—he ruled for thirty-six years—showed only that Persia was in danger of being destroyed. Violently ambitious himself, Fath Ali Shah had to contend with the violent ambitions of Napoleon and Tsar Paul of Russia, both of whom planned expeditions against Persia, the Tsar even going so far as to order his Cossacks to march from one end of Persia to the other, an order which they refused to obey.

It was the time when the European powers were attempting to carve up Asia, as later they were to carve up Africa. Napoleon urged the Shah to make war on Russia and recover Georgia as an ally of the French: the Shah was still contemplating war with Russia when Napoleon went down to defeat. Thereafter, the British and the Russians contended for mastery.

Under Nasir-ud-Din, who came to the throne in 1848, British influence predominated, and for the first

THE SPLENDOR OF PERSIA

time, Persia began to experiment with western ideas. Hospitals were built. Engineers were sent abroad to be trained, and the Shah himself paid two visits to Europe. In his reign there appeared the last of the great series of visionary prophets who, from time to time, have fired the imaginations of the Persians.

A certain Ali Mohammad, the son of a grocer, born in Shiraz in 1820, announced that he was the long-promised *Bab* or "Gate," by which mankind would be united with the twelfth Imam of the Shia sect. He appeared at Shiraz on May 23, 1844, exactly one thousand years after the disappearance of the Twelfth Imam. He claimed to be even greater than the Prophet Mohammad; he called himself "the Highest" and "He who arises from the House of the Prophet at the end of time." He described himself as the mirror in which men might see God. With astonishing astuteness he combined elements of Zoroastrianism with elements of Islam. He issued edicts as though he were King, Emperor, and Archpriest. All Persia trembled before the power of this man who seemed possessed of super-natural gifts. Women flocked to him. Jailed, he succeeded in escaping, and the governor of Isfahan offered him hospitality. The Shah issued orders to stamp out the movement. There were battles near Meshed. By August 1849 the Shah realized that the movement was so strong that he possessed no physical means of putting an end to it. Accordingly, he induced the Babis to surrender on the promise of an amnesty, then he massacred them. The *Bab* was captured. In the great square

THE AWAKENING

of Tabriz the man who claimed to be God was blind-folded, bound hand and foot and set up against a wall. When the smoke cleared after the first volley of the firing party, there was no sign of him—the shots had cut his ropes and he had fled. The miracle of his dis-appearance was explained a few days later when he was found in a guard-room by one of his own followers, who shot him out of hand.

The martyr dead, the movement of the Babis had only just begun. All Persia flared with insurrections. An attempt was made on the life of the Shah. Captured Babis were put to death by being buried upside down or placed within stone pillars where they suffocated to death. A successor to the dead *Bab* appeared, calling himself "the Morning of Eternity." Gradually the movement began to lose its impetus within the borders of Persia; the surviving Babis escaped to Turkey. To-day on Mount Carmel one can visit the astonishing temple and splendid gardens belonging to the Babis, who now call themselves Bahaists.

When the long reign of Nasir-ud-Din ended with his assassination in 1896, the influence of western ideas had only barely penetrated. Persia had a postal service, a bank, a handful of foreign doctors, a precarious tele-graph system, and currency modelled on European coinage. It was still, however, a mediaeval monarchy. "I want ministers," the Shah said once, "who do not know whether Brussels is a capital or a cabbage." He got them. His son, Muzaffar-ud-Din, who succeeded him, was forced to call a *Majlis* or Parliament, but suffering a stroke immediately after the convocation of the Majlis, he watched power falling into the hands of a violently reactionary Grand Vizier determined to put an end to parliamentary rule. When Muzaffar-ud-Din died, the treasury was empty, the Majlis was powerless and the new Shah, Mohammad Ali, was determined to wield absolute power over a rebellious people. The battle between the Majlis and the Shah ended in victory for the people, with the Shah escaping into the compound of the Russian Legation, begging for asylum; then he faded into obscurity, only to appear briefly in the summer of 1911 at the head of a small royalist army which landed on the shores of the Caspian and attempted a march to Teheran. His forces were routed. In his place at the head of the government was the regent, Nasir-ul-Mulk, the redoubtable adviser to Nasir-ud-Din.

In the years when western ideas were beginning to penetrate the country, it was the fate of Persia to find herself at the mercy of fierce pressures from abroad. American influence became widespread, largely as a result of the work of Morgan Schuster who with immense energy began to put the nation's finances in order. The gendarmerie was placed under the command of Swedes. It was hoped that, by employing Americans and Scandinavians a way might be found to avoid falling under the domination of either Great Britain or Russia. Inevitably there were confusions. The birth-pangs of the new state lasted well into the twentieth century.

THE AWAKENING

✛✛✛✛✛✛✛✛

AT THE END of the First World War, Persia was still weak and desperate for guidance, while nominally under the rule of Ahmad Shah. Bolshevik, White Russian, and British forces had fought over the northern stretches of the country. In this extremity, the country in a state of chaos, a certain Reza Khan, the son of an army officer from Mazanderan on the shores of the Caspian, took over the effective government, having marched 2,500 men to Teheran and thrown the government into a panic of fear. He appointed himself war minister and commander-in-chief, and set about welding the army into a powerful striking force. Handsome, swarthy, thick-set, with a mind like a sharp flint, and an absolute lack of inhibitions in the methods he employed to reshape the country closer to his desire, he deliberately concealed his power. He made and unmade premiers, but refused to accept the trappings of supreme power until he felt that the people were ripe for dictatorship. In 1923 his army swept into Teheran and he assumed the premiership. In the following year the Shah was sent into exile, and a year later the obscure officer of the Cossack Division was appointed Shah of Persia and the sovereignty was vested in his family. He assumed the ancient name of Pahlavi. The task he gave himself was nothing less than to revive the ancient virtues of the Persians and at the same time to transform Persia into a modern state.

Within a decade he had repaired the errors of cen-

THE SPLENDOR OF PERSIA

turies of misrule. He set the parliament to work, built
railways—it was said that he simply drew a line across
the map of Persia to indicate where he wanted the railways to be laid—issued orders for the abolition of the
white face-veil worn by Persian women (they still wear
it), and set about reorganizing schools, agricultural colleges, and universities. He attempted to settle the no-
mads, those great migratory tribes whose power arose
from the implicit obedience of the tribesmen to their
khans. He learned much from Mustapha Kemal, who
was busily remoulding the Turks, but he was guided
most by his instinctive knowledge of what was possible.
He could be, and often was, merciless to those who dis-
obeyed him, but for the first time since the reign of
Shah Abbas, the Persians were able to give undivided
respect to their ruler. If his dictatorial methods created
resentment, his successful reforms won the affection of
the people.

In the Second World War, the Axis Powers attempted to capture Persia from within. The German
Legation became an overstaffed spy centre. The British
and the Russians, suspecting the Shah of undue tolerance to German intrigue, decided to act quickly, fear-
ing that the Germans, already in the Caucasus, would
be able to join up with the tribesmen who had already
proclaimed loyalty to the Axis. In August 1942, British
and Russian forces, acting simultaneously, entered
Persia and the Shah was deposed in favor of his son,
Prince Mohammad Reza Pahlavi, then a young man of
twenty-two. The former Shah died in Johannesburg

THE AWAKENING

two years later, broken-hearted and still claiming his right to the throne.

With the coming to the throne of the new Shah, Persia entered a new dispensation. His father had been a dictator; the son was determined to rule as a constitutional monarch but, at the same time, he was determined to influence the conduct of affairs. He insisted that his orders be carried out, but without ruthlessness. A skilled pilot, he had affection for machines. An expert farmer, he was close to the peasants. He, too, possessed an instinctive knowledge of the possible. And if his greatest virtue was his democratic temper, his greatest contribution to Persia was, and is, his knowledge of his own country and the use he has made of this knowledge. Under the young Shah, the splendor of ancient Persia is being revived.

THE SPLENDOR OF PERSIA

About the Author

IN THE SPRING of 1949, Robert Payne made an extensive visit to Persia. Since then he has been in frequent touch with Persian scholars and with visitors from Persia and has become a devoted student of Persian history and a staunch admirer of Persian art and literature.

Born in Saltash, Cornwall, England, Mr. Payne was educated at the Universities of Cape Town and Liverpool and at The Sorbonne. He has held teaching posts at the Universities of Fuhtan in Chungking and Lienta in Kunming and has been a Professor of English at Alabama College in the United States.

Mr. Payne is the author of over forty books, many of which are about Asia or with Asian background. He is widely known as a novelist, and his short stories and articles have appeared in numerous magazines and newspapers.

Of *Splendor of Persia*, Mr. Payne says: "I wanted to set down quite simply an account of the Persian splendor—that dazzling and continuing richness which has come out of a country already old when Greece was young. I wanted the readers to be able to see the Achaemenians, Sasanians and Seljuks walking before their eyes. There is a flamelit barbaric gentleness in the works of the Persian artists and poets, and I think this too should have its place in any account of Persia. And then in various ways—in the building of our cathedrals, in our language, in our art and even in our fairy tales—we owe so much to Persia that there is a good deal to be said for stating the debt clearly.

"Above all, I wanted to tell the story of Persia as one great sweeping panorama in which Xerxes, Darius, Tamerlane and all the rest are seen as part of a still-living tradition."